Cousins
and
The Death of Papa

Cousins

and

The Death of Papa

HORTON FOOTE

*The Final Two Plays of The
Orphans' Home Cycle*

with an Introduction by
Samuel G. Freedman

Grove Press
New York

The introduction appeared in a slightly different form in *The New York Times Magazine* on February 9, 1986, and is reprinted by permission. The author wishes to express his gratitude to Gerald Walker, who edited the original article.

Library of Congress Cataloging-in-Publication Data

Foote, Horton.
Cousins; and, the Death of Papa: the final two plays of The orphans' home cycle/Horton Foote; with an introduction by Samuel G. Freedman.
p. cm.

ISBN-13: 978-0-8021-3152-2

1. Title: Cousins. II. Title: Death of Papa.
PS3511.O344C7 1999
812—dc19   88-26071

Design by Irving Perkins Associates
Manufactured in the United States of America

Grove Press
an imprint of Grove/Atlantic, Inc.
841 Broadway
New York, NY 10003

Distributed by Publishers Group West

www.groveatlantic.com

09 10 11 12   10 9 8 7 6 5 4 3 2

*For Lillian
and my grandmother,
Daisy Speed Brooks*

Contents

Introduction

HORTON FOOTE STEPS out of his car and through the iron
gates of the cemetery in Wharton, Texas, his hometown.
He is looking for his grandfather's grave. It is a raw winter
afternoon, the sky low and gray, the air damp. But Horton
Foote is not melancholy. Here, he is a man surrounded by
friends, by people he knew, by the characters who popu-
late his plays and films. The route to his grandfather's plot
is circuitous, constantly interrupted by the sight of a
familiar name etched in granite.

"I love these old tombstones," says Foote, the gulf wind
tousling his white hair and rippling his blue blazer. "My
grandfather died when I was nine and my grandmother
was in mourning for two years. I was very fond of her, and
every afternoon we'd go out for a drive with her chauf-
feur. First, we'd go and see how the cotton crop was. Then
we'd come here. She'd bring flowers and sometimes she'd
sit and cry. I always felt at home here."

He points to a seven-foot-tall tablet. "The Dawdy ladies
taught Sunday school when I was a kid." Further ahead,
he nods toward the bust of a woman, her marble hair
fixed eternally in a bun. "The Crooms, they're kin to me."
He sighs, laughs a little, and confesses, "When I came
back for a visit two years ago, someone said, 'Let's throw a
party for Horton.' And someone else said, 'Where, in the
graveyard?' I know more people here than I know alive."

Going to the graveyard is more than an exercise in memory. From the cemetery, from Wharton itself, has come the artistry of Horton Foote—his characters, his conflicts, his language, his themes. He left Wharton fifty-six years ago, when he was sixteen, and yet he returns again and again, like some animal answering instinct; and when he is not in Wharton in the flesh, he is there in imagination. For the half-century of his career, Foote has set every original play, novel, and screenplay in Wharton, from *The Traveling Lady* to *Tender Mercies*, from *The Chase* to *The Trip to Bountiful*. To contemplate Foote is, above all, to contemplate the symbiosis between writer and place. Even when Foote has adapted the work of other writers— Harper Lee's *To Kill a Mockingbird*, William Faulkner's "Old Man" and "Tomorrow," even Betty Bao Lord's Chinese family epic *Spring Moon*—the psychic terrain has seemed as much his as theirs.

Foote for too long remained a relative secret in American literature—a writer's writer—because of his withdrawal from New York and Hollywood for a twenty-year period beginning in the mid-1960s. Even in his current flurry of activity, Foote's words offer a private kind of pleasure, much like the scrubby, flat landscape of Wharton in winter, ordinary to the itinerant eye, but oddly beautiful for one who lingers. If the tight aperture of Foote's vision has its critics, who find there a stasis and a sameness, it also has earned him champions and honors, notably Academy Awards for the screenplays of *Tender Mercies* and *To Kill a Mockingbird* and an Academy Award nomination for *The Trip to Bountiful*. When Geraldine Page won the Best Actress Oscar for her performance in the film, she paid Foote tribute in her acceptance speech.

The production and publication of the nine plays comprising the *Orphans' Home Cycle*, Foote's family saga, guarantees him a deservedly permanent place in American letters. As of this writing, *Lily Dale, The Widow Claire, 1918, Courtship, Valentine's Day,* and *Cousins* have received stagings in both commercial and nonprofit theaters from Los Angeles to New York. Adaptations of *1918* and *Valentine's Day* (released as *On Valentine's Day*) have reached the screen, *Roots in a Parched Ground* and *Convicts* are in the process of being filmed, and *Lily Dale* and *The Widow Claire* appear likely to follow. With a three-book set, culminating in this volume, Grove Press has brought into print the entire cycle. *Cousins* and *The Death of Papa*, the two plays collected here, find Horace and Elizabeth Robedaux, the fictive reincarnations of Foote's own parents, grappling with the infirmity and the demise of their own elders, events with resonance far beyond the familial. *The Death of Papa* also places onstage for the first time in the cycle Horace Jr., the author's alter ego. He is a relentlessly inquisitive lad; he is, quite clearly, a writer in the making, and also a human being.

"I believe very deeply in the human spirit, and I have a sense of awe about it," Foote says in the living room of his Wharton home, his frequent retreat from a Manhattan apartment. "Because I don't know how people carry on. I look around and I ask, What makes the difference in people? What is it?

"I've known people the world has thrown everything at—to discourage them, to kill them, to break their spirit. And yet something about them retains a dignity. They face life and they don't ask quarters. Look at the blacks, my God. Or there's my great-aunt Nanny—widowed, four children, living on the charity of her brother, never had anything. Yet she always had dignity, never complained. You always wanted her around, always went to her for comfort, for solace. I've just seen example after example of people enduring things I absolutely couldn't. I'm always measuring myself. Could I do that? Could I take that?"

Yet Foote, faced with futility, has measured up, much like Horace Robedaux of the *Orphans' Home Cycle*, much like Mac Sledge, the country singer seeking redemption in *Tender Mercies*. After building a career for twenty-five years on Broadway, in Hollywood and for such television shows as "Playhouse 90," Foote virtually vanished for a generation. His closest collaborators among producers and directors—Joseph Anthony, Fred Coe, Vincent Donehue, Mary Hunter—had died, retired or changed direction by the mid-1960s. Amid the avant-garde theater movement, Foote found his name suddenly unknown and his subtle style out of favor. He moved his family from Nyack, New York, to rural New Hampshire in 1966 and, at his lowest, he considered putting down his pen. Then, again like Mac Sledge, Foote found strength and perseverance through a woman, his wife.

"I'd often talk about finding something else to do," Foote remembers. "Lillian was selling real estate and we both loved antiques and sometimes I'd say, 'Maybe I'll open an antiques shop.' She'd always say, 'Stick to the writing.' She never doubted it. We'd get in the car and I'd say, 'Lillian, I can't stand the theater, the state it's in. I can't stand Hollywood. I have no talent as a novelist. I love poetry but it's not my form. I'm stuck with plays, and what am I doing? What's going to happen?' And she kept me goin'. She never lost faith, and that's a rare thing. I don't know how we got through it, but we got through it." He beams across the room to Lillian. "Didn't we, darlin'?"

Catalyzed by the death of both parents, and urged on by Lillian, Foote kept writing, sitting in New England with the wood stove burning, and turning relentlessly back to Wharton and childhood, like Quentin Compson in Faulkner's *Absalom, Absalom!* hunched in a Harvard dormitory, but telling tales of Yoknapatawpha County. In a two-year span, Foote wrote the entire nine-play cycle, with the exception of *The Widow Claire*. His work found passionate patrons in Peggy Feury, the highly respected acting instructor, and Herbert Berghof, a director, acting teacher, and longtime friend—and, through them, noncommercial theaters such as the Ensemble Studio Theater in Manhattan and the Actors Theater of Louisville and commercial producers like Lewis Allen and Philip Hobel.

So began Foote's re-emergence. He followed the *Orphans' Home Cycle* by writing *Tender Mercies* for his friend Robert Duvall, and the film won Oscars for both of them in 1983. Two years later, Foote had both a play, *The Road to the Graveyard,* and a film, *The Trip to Bountiful* (based on his 1953 play), named by *The New York Times's* critics to their ten-best lists. Since then, unceasing activity has carried Foote from research in China to film locations in Texas to directing duties in Pittsburgh. At the age of seventy-two, he is a man reborn.

"In a curious way, in a seemingly undramatic way, Horton is a remarkable person," says the director and producer Alan J. Pakula, a friend for more than twenty years. "He has a specific voice, a specific style, and he has never abandoned it, even though it has cost him. He has never cut his talent to the fashion of the time. And because he wrote his plays, whether they were going to be produced or not, he got what most American writers don't get—a second act. You are seeing continuity and fruition now, because he never wavered from his vision."

* * *

Horton and Lillian Foote are eating lunch at a barbecue joint on the outskirts of Wharton, a town of 9,000 about fifty-five miles southwest of Houston. "There's a time when I would've known everybody here," Horton says wistfully. "Now I'm lookin' around and there's not a one I know."

In his life, and in his letters, Foote is preoccupied with change, with the erosion of tradition and identity. He has seen it in Wharton, where franchises, tract houses, and garden apartments spill across the cotton fields while the old downtown corrodes. When Foote drives down West Milam Street, the bustling shopping street where his father ran a clothing store, all he finds on a Saturday afternoon is two girls collecting money for the high-school band. Richmond Road, once a gravel lane shaded by oaks and sycamores, now is a strip of asphalt flanked by Jack in the Box and the Kwik Kar Wash. There hasn't been a good place in town to get grits and greens since Lavania's closed a few years ago. The ironic result is that even as Foote set *1918, Valentine's Day,* and *The Trip to Bountiful* in and around Wharton, all had to be filmed in the north Texas town of Waxahachie.

"This could be nine million towns in America," Foote says as he drives. "Could be anywhere."

The demise of his hometown, wrenching yet inevitable, resounds through Foote's work. What Brooks Atkinson said in 1941 of *Texas Town,* Foote's first full-length play, could apply equally well to such recent works as *The Road to the Graveyard* and *The Habitation of Dragons:* "His play gives a real and languid impression of a town changing in its relation to the world—the old stock drifting down the economic and social scale, the young people at loose ends."

The *Orphans' Home Cycle* starts in 1902 with the death of Horace Robedaux's father and ends in 1928 with the death of Elizabeth's, each event shattering a family. The subtext of the cycle is a larger upheaval: the fall of the plantation aristocracy and the ascent of a mercantile class, its own fortunes uneasily dependent on the cotton crop. When Elizabeth Robedaux says in *Valentine's Day*, "I want everything to stay the way it is," she is uttering the one prayer Foote refuses to answer.

Such images of loss spring from one dominant memory, the memory that most especially animates *The Death of Papa*. "The event that always stuck with me, the event I've always been groping toward as a writer, was the day my grandfather died," Foote says. "Until then, life was just magic. I never felt so secure in my life as sitting on the porch swing and knowing I was the grandson of one of the richest families in town and my grandfather was the most respected man in town.

"One day, I came home from school and the house was silent and my mother was away. This puzzled me. I went over to play with my friend and his mother said, 'Son, you better get to your grandmother's.' And she didn't tell me why. I went into the backyard and Liza and Sarah, these two black women, were there and they saw me and they were crying. And I heard Liza say she knew something was going to happen because there'd been a dove on the house that morning.

"I went into the long back hall and my mother came up to me and she was in a dark dress. She said, 'Do you want to see your grandmother?' And I said, 'Yes, I do.' I went into her bedroom and my grandfather's coffin was there. She was over his coffin, just sobbing. My mother said, 'Little Horton is here,' and my grandmother just looked up and . . ." He never finishes the sentence. "I think it was the turning point to my whole family. He was kind of the king. And from then on, we had many problems that he would've shielded us from. He was just such a symbol."

But while Foote mourns the passage of familiar things, of the certainty embodied by his grandfather, he is no Norman Rockwell. He looks back, as Alan J. Pakula puts it, "with compassion and astringence." Stillbirth, influenza, alcoholism, and madness afflict his characters. Parents disown their children, brothers compete for political office and cuckolds kill adulterers. Nor does Foote endorse the social order of his childhood, the almost Confucian set of hierarchies that governed life and even death, with separate cemeteries for whites, blacks, and Mexicans.

Foote, after all, was the son of parents who had eloped when his maternal grandparents objected to the marriage. They were political rebels as well. His mother, Hallie, voted as a liberal Democrat in a town of decidedly conservative bent. His father, Albert Horton Foote, survived as a shopkeeper on business from local blacks, raising civic suspicion about his racial loyalties, a theme running through both *Cousins* and *The Death of Papa*. Young Horton's ambition to become an actor also set him outside the social orbit of Wharton, and he left his hometown at sixteen.

His path led from acting studies in Dallas and Pasadena, California, to summer stock on Martha's Vineyard to membership in New York's American Actors Company, for which he began writing plays. While Foote the actor got savaged by critics, Foote the author received encouraging reviews. The young Texan, who had promised himself Broadway stardom by the age of 24, suddenly found himself a New York playwright instead. Yet Foote never went longer than two years without a visit home, and, until her death in 1974, his mother wrote to him every single day. Several years ago, he bought the house in which he was raised.

"This is why I keep coming back here," Foote says. "It's so fluid in some ways, so rigid in some ways. No matter how far away I've been—New York, London, Hollywood—half of me is always thinking about Wharton, trying to figure out some aspect of this life back here. I mean, I have social points of view that are not shared by a lot of people, but I never picked fights much. I listened to them and tried to understand what made them feel the way they did. Not that I've ever understood, but I've learned to listen. I'm a social writer in the sense that I want to record, but not in the sense of trying to change people's minds."

Somehow all the opposing currents—empathy and rejection, elegy, and good riddance—coalesce in one story. "See that pecan tree up yonder?" Foote asks, pointing out the living-room window. "When my grandfather gave his land to the city, there was a pecan tree bigger than that on it. There was a gentleman's understanding they'd never cut that tree down. And five years after he died, they came out with their axes and cut the tree down. Well, part of me says I don't understand not honoring things ancient, things like trees, families. And part of me says I don't believe in the aristocracy."

In the small world of Wharton, and in the measured tone of Foote's writing, the fall of a family takes on almost

Biblical proportions. One afternoon, Foote drives to the cemetery on the plantation once owned by a governor. What were 2,200 acres of prime bottom land are now a mix of suburban ranch houses and untended fields. Within a rusted metal fence, weeds and saplings have overgrown the little graveyard. The few tombstones are tilted and cracked. "Let this," Foote says as he turns to leave, "be a lesson in humility."

*   *   *

That evening, Foote visits his aunt, Laura Ray. She lives in a garden-apartment complex of vaguely Castillian appointments, a frail woman tended by her son. But her mind is sharp, filled with memories, and Foote has come to plumb them. A septuagenarian himself, in Aunt Laura's company he suddenly reverts to the role of inquiring nephew, eyes gleaming as she remembers the old days. Aunt Laura talks about almost being thrown out of church for the sin of playing bridge; she recalls the relative from Galveston who snored and the kitchen helper named Charity who was a conjurer; she speaks of picnics on the Brazos River and afternoons at Outlar's Drugstore. "It didn't seem dull at the time," she says.

Such encounters have fed Foote's imagination since childhood. One of the particular pleasures of *The Death of Papa* is the appearance of Horace Robedaux, Jr., a character who like his creator exhibits a limitless curiosity and an exquisite ear. "When I was growing up," Foote says, "I spent half of my time in the house listening. I always loved old people, and you know they always adored me, because I could sit and listen for hours. Ask 'em this, that, get 'em off on tangents. Often, I'd go home and mimic them for my mother. And I always wanted to go back for more."

He goes back now with an author's acuity. "It's the

minutiae that fascinate me," Foote says. "I have this obsessive interest in the details of people. I can sit and listen to nine hundred different people down here. I don't get bored. I don't have to be intellectually stimulated." Hallie Foote remembers that when her father worked in Hollywood on screenplays, he rarely socialized with the film colony but always got to know the hotel maids because "they had the stories."

The act of writing starts with a similar attention to detail. "There's an exercise actors do," Foote says. "If you want to recall an emotion from the past, instead of fixing on the emotion you try to remember specific things, like the odor in the room at the time or the color of the wallpaper. Those kinds of things invite emotion." When he hits a snag, Foote often goes out driving with his wife. "There are times," Lillian Foote says, "when I'll look over and see him making little gestures with his hand, working out the things he'll write. I see him the same way around the house sometimes. I know something is happening even before the writing begins."

Lillian Foote's presence is also felt in Foote's female characters, from Georgette Thomas in *The Traveling Lady* to Elizabeth Robedaux in the *Orphans' Home Cycle*. "There's a kind of woman my father always writes—gentle but very strong," Hallie Foote says. "Often, they seem dependent on the man, but they exhibit this strength. These women survive and they do it with dignity. Rosa Lee in *Tender Mercies* is sort of fearless. She could allay the fears in Mac. And that's how my mother is. She believes so completely in my father and his talent. It's almost like she had a plan for him. She's the rock, she's the rock."

The key to Foote's writing, the signature of his style, is his ability to convey both melodramatic events and loqua-

cious language in a spare, reductive manner. While his
plots suggest Faulkner, his style is reminiscent of
Katherine Anne Porter, and his mastery of subtext is
closer to that of a work as seemingly different as *The Car
Thief,* Theodore Weesner's novel of working-class Michi-
gan, than to anything from the Southern Gothic tradition. Foote is influenced primarily by poetry, the most
skeletal of forms, and by music. The composer Charles
Ives has affected Foote with his use of multiple themes—
similar to the thickly woven plots in the *Orphans' Home
Cycle*—and his fondness for "found music." Music plays
an organic and highly suggestive role throughout Foote's
work, from the hymns in *The Trip to Bountiful* to the nor-
teno waltzes in *The Road to the Graveyard.* These songs,
rather than comprising a calculated soundtrack, are the
pastels on Foote's palette.

Foote's approach to writing does not vary widely
between films and plays, which may explain why his
movies bear such a personal stamp. In an age when the
lexicon of cinema is largely visual, Foote stresses dialogue
and character development rather than spectacle or even
traditional narrative. The major events in the film adaptation of *Valentine's Day*—a local bank faltering, the town
eccentric committing suicide, a daughter reconciling with
her parents—do not propel the plot as much as they create
a mood. In transforming stage play into screenplay, Foote
resisted the temptation to broadly "open up" the story,
substituting a few visual sequences outdoors for what
was living-room exposition on stage instead. "The difference with a screenplay," Foote says, "is that right away I
know I have the luxury of saying, 'I can go here, I can go
there.' The challenge is that the story not disperse itself.
There's a kind of debauchery that happens to directors—

'We'll make this interesting by finding an interesting place for it.' I find many films today boring because they're all visually conceived."

Foote's technique is to pour out everything in his first drafts, then edit harshly. At one point in *Tender Mercies*, for instance, Mac Sledge attends the funeral of his daughter, who has been killed in an auto accident. Foote initially wrote a three-page scene in which Rosa Lee and her son, who have been nervously chattering, meet a taciturn Sledge at the Dallas airport. Foote scrapped the entire passage. The airport, he decided, was too impersonal a setting for a key scene. The chitchat between Rosa Lee and her son, meant to establish that they were uneasy about Mac's return, did not seem central to the scene. The heart of it, Foote decided, had to be Mac's reaction to the funeral. Mac, then, had to do the talking in the scene, and yet he had to retain his inward, stoic personality.

On a later draft of the screenplay, Foote moved directly from the funeral to Sledge and Rosa Lee working in their garden, a very personal place. Rosa Lee asks Mac what's wrong. In a one-paragraph speech, he quietly lists the early deaths he has seen. The speech closes with a line Foote inserted on the rewrite: "I don't trust happiness. I never did. I never will." In its matter-of-fact way, the passage is the sound of a man railing against an arbitrary universe.

Foote's determination to keep the emotional flame low, dramatic as the surrounding events may be, deeply divides critics and audiences. At his very best, Foote creates "an unbearable turbulence beneath that tranquil surface," as drama critic of *The New York Times*, Frank Rich, once put it. But while *The Trip to Bountiful* made the ten-best lists of several critics, Richard Schickel in *Time* magazine dismissed it as "all fragile moods and memories," an "essentially empty drama." And the problem is commercial as much as critical. Twenty years apart, studios balked at distributing both *To Kill a Mockingbird* and *Tender Mercies* until each built word-of-mouth support through screenings.

Foote, normally accommodating to a fault, bridles at the criticism (or faint praise) of his work as "soft" or "small." In a 1985 interview with Foote, Lynn Neary of National Public Radio called *The Trip to Bountiful* "a simple story, a small story." Foote shot back that he preferred the word "personal," because, "I think 'small' denigrates it." Neary said she didn't mean "small" as a fault. "But you know the industry feels that way about it," Foote answered. "This is a personal battle of mine."

"All I can tell you is that I follow my instincts," Foote said. "I've tried to be more theatrical, more sensational. It's not my style. It's not my sense of truth. For instance, I admire Shakespeare greatly and deeply love to read him, but his is not my favorite type of theater. Often it embarrasses me and also I don't believe a lot of it."

For collaborators as well as critics, Foote's work is a take-it-or-leave-it proposition. "You've got to be careful," Robert Duvall says. "You can't make too many false moves with his writing. You can't push it. You can't propel it along. You have to just let it lay there. It's like rural Chekhov, simple but deep." The director Herbert Berghof adds: "The beauty of Horton's work is that it is all his. If you want to tamper with it, it cannot be done."

Nor is Foote inclined to allow tampering. This paunchy Southern gentleman, who drinks Dr Pepper and eats milk toast, will fight when cornered. "The old Southern saying, 'You catch more flies with honey than with vinegar' is very much how Horton works," says Ken Harrison, the director of *1918* and *On Valentine's Day.* "But when the honey doesn't work, Horton does whatever he has to to get what he wants. He can be tenacious." In the case of *On Valentine's Day*, Foote functioned almost as a co-director. He helped Harrison rehearse the cast in New York before location shooting began, he was on the set frequently making notes, and he shared the editing decisions with the director.

In all of his recent plays and films, Foote has relied on family, both literal and figurative. Lillian Foote, with or without a title, has been Horton's most regular editor, sounding board and *chargé d'affaires.* Their children Hallie and Horton, Jr., acted in both *1918* and *On Valentine's Day,* and Hallie starred opposite Matthew Broderick in the superb Circle in the Square production of *The Widow Claire.* (Another daughter, Daisy, is a writer, and another son, Walter, is a lawyer.) Peter Masterson, the director of *The Trip to Bountiful,* is Foote's cousin. Geraldine Page, the star of the film, appeared in Foote's teleplay of "Old Man," in 1957. Foote discovered Robert Duvall at the Neighborhood Playhouse in 1955 and arranged to have him cast as Boo Radley in *To Kill a Mockingbird,* Duvall's first break. Since then Duvall has appeared in Foote's play and film of the Faulkner short story "Tomorrow," as well as in *Tender Mercies,* and he will star in the forthcoming film adaptation of *Convicts.*

The reason Foote inspires such loyalty, Duvall suggests, is simple: "It's his writing. If he didn't write the way he does, I don't know if we'd be loyal."

But in Foote's case, fidelity is more a personal trait than a professional ploy. He has been married to the same woman for forty-three years. He has had only one agent,

Lucy Kroll, for nearly forty-five years. Wharton embraces Foote not so much for his achievements—*1918* was not even stocked at Wharton's video-cassette store a year after its release—as for his faithfulness.

During a December 1985 visit to Wharton, for instance, Foote went to see Catherine Davis, a black woman who worked in his mother's household for generations. She is in her nineties now, a shrunken woman in a red housecoat and a blue wool hat, living in a hut of tar paper, plywood, and corrugated cardboard. But this hovel is what she owns in the world and, so much like one of Foote's heroine survivors, she makes it a home, covering the walls with snapshots of grandchildren, a calendar showing Negro League baseball stars and, protected under cellophane, a picture of John and Jackie Kennedy.

Foote asked Catherine Davis about her health. She asked him about Hallie. As their time came to an end, the old woman said, "It's good y'all come back." She pointed a bony finger at Foote. "Come back, come back, come back."

And Foote will, in the most permanent sense. A few years ago, his brother John called him and said there was only one plot left in the Wharton cemetery, where their parents and grandparents lay. Foote bought it for $200. Even at seventy-two, hardly a young man, nothing in the purchase or in the finality it represents depressed him. Death is just another way of going home.

"This is a sweet old graveyard," Foote had said among the tombstones that cold winter day. "How could anybody be scared to be out here?"

Samuel G. Freedman
November, 1988

Cousins

Characters

HORACE ROBEDAUX

GORDON KIRBY

LEWIS HIGGINS

ELIZABETH ROBEDAUX

HENRY VAUGHN

WILL KIDDER

MONTY REEVES

LOLA REEVES

PETE DAVENPORT

CORELLA DAVENPORT

LILY DALE KIDDER

NURSE

SYLVESTER MALONE

MINNIE CURTIS

Place: Harrison, Texas
Houston, Texas
Time: 1925

The lights come up on a section of Horace Robedaux's men's store. We see a table stacked with men's slacks. HORACE stands in front of the table. It is raining. He listens to the rain and watches the sidewalk and the street in front of the store.

From time to time he sings a phrase or two of "Let Me Call You Sweetheart," interrupts his singing with a sigh, then continues singing. After a beat, he walks behind the table and begins to rearrange the pants. GORDON KIRBY, Horace's cousin and clerk, comes in.

GORDON: Well, Cousin Horace, I have been up and down the streets and none of the stores are doing any business. I saw Mr. Harris and Mr. Davis in the drugstore having coffee. And Mr. Randolph and Mr. Burton are standing out in front of their stores and all their clerks are just standing around, too. I guess you are glad you only have one clerk. What if you had to pay the salary of eight or nine, like Mr. Davis? (*Pause.*) Cousin Horace?

HORACE: Yes . . .

GORDON: What can I do?

HORACE: Nothing. We'll just wait for some customers.

GORDON: I've got to go over in an hour and pick up the posters for my dance I'm giving in two weeks. Then in the afternoon, if you don't mind, I'll distribute a few of the posters around town. I should do pretty well on this one. The Blue Blazers are going to play for me and they can be very popular. I'm charging seventy-five cents a couple this time. For my dance last month I charged a dollar and a quarter per couple and nobody came. I lost thirty dollars on the night. I can't say nobody came. Eleven couples came. But you can't make money on a dance if only eleven couples come, especially when the orchestra and the hall and the printing all cost.

(HORACE *sighs. It is a loud sigh, almost a groan.* GORDON *looks up at him.*)

Did you say something, Cousin Horace?

HORACE: No.

GORDON: I thought you said something.

HORACE: No.

GORDON: Not even my kinfolks come to my dance. I said to Mama this morning: "What's the matter with our kin-folks? You'd think you could count on your kinfolks. Wouldn't you?" I mean look at all our cousins. You'd think kinfolks would stick together. Cousin Lewis came. But he was drunk and he tried to start a fight like he always does. (*Pause.*) I swear Cousin Lewis hasn't learned anything. I mean he killed Jamie Dale, cut him in cold blood. And because he was drunk and Jamie Dale was drunk they let him off with a suspended sentence, which he pays no attention to and walks around day and night always at least half full, carrying a knife or a gun until I know and you know he will kill somebody else or get killed. (*Pause.*) Don't you agree? (*Pause.*) Cousin Horace?

HORACE: What?

GORDON: Don't you agree?

HORACE: Agree about what? I'm sorry, I wasn't listening.

GORDON: About Cousin Lewis.

HORACE: What about him?

GORDON: He hasn't learned anything from his trial and suspended sentence.

HORACE: I don't know.

GORDON: I don't think he has. Jamie Dale was his cousin, too, wasn't he?

HORACE: Whose?

GORDON: Cousin Lewis Higgins.

HORACE: Yes. They were cousins.

GORDON: But Jamie Dale wasn't our cousin.

HORACE: No.

GORDON: How are they cousins?

HORACE: Who?

GORDON: Jamie Dale and Cousin Lewis Higgins.

HORACE: I don't know. I knew once but I've forgotten. I believe on Lewis's father's side.

GORDON: Cousin Lewis is my second cousin and your second cousin, isn't that right?

HORACE: Yes. (*Pause.*) No. Second cousin, once removed.

GORDON: Oh. Is that how it is? (*Pause.*) You and I are first cousins.

HORACE: Yes.

GORDON: I was figuring up the other day. I have eleven first cousins on my mother's side, and at least fifty second cousins, and God knows how many fourth and fifth cousins. Somebody is always turning up and saying: "You know we're cousins?" My mother and your mother . . . (*Pause. He laughs.*) We are kin to a lot of people, Cousin Horace. That's on my mother's side and your mother's side. I don't know much about my daddy's people. You keep up with your daddy's people, don't you?

HORACE: In a way.

GORDON: They're spread all over the state, aren't they?

HORACE: Yes.

GORDON: Some of them are in Houston?

HORACE: Yes.

GORDON: Cousin Lily Dale has married a real smart man, everyone says. He's really a good businessman. I call him Cousin Will, too. They have a pretty new house, but that's not good enough for Cousin Will, Cousin Lily Dale says, and he's selling it and buying them a big new house. A two-story brick house. (*Pause.*) How's Aunt Corella's health?

HORACE: I think it's pretty fair.

GORDON: Will she have to have this other operation?

HORACE: I haven't heard.

GORDON: How many operations has she had in all?

HORACE: Three.

GORDON: All serious, too?

HORACE: Pretty serious.

GORDON: And I bet they cost a lot. Those Houston doctors are expensive.

HORACE: I guess so.

GORDON: When I go to Houston in the fall to night school I'm going to live with them. Of course, I'm going to pay board and room. Mama says it will help them out a lot. She says it's been hard on them, Aunt Corella having so many operations. (*Pause.*) I like Cousin Pete, although he doesn't have a great deal to say. Mama likes him, too. He calls her "Widow." He's always asking her when she's going to marry again. (*Pause.*) I call him "Cousin Pete," although he's my uncle by marriage. What do you call him?

HORACE: Mr. Davenport.

GORDON: What do your children call him?

HORACE: Uncle Pete.

GORDON (*laughing*): Uncle Pete? They call him Uncle Pete and he's their stepgrandfather. And you call him Mr. Davenport and he's your stepfather and I call him Cousin Pete and he's my uncle by marriage. (*He laughs again.*) He worships Cousin Lily Dale, Mama says, always has.

(*Pause.*) Did you live with them when you were in Houston at business school?

HORACE: No. I stayed in the same boarding house as my Cousin Minnie.

GORDON: Who's Cousin Minnie? Is she my cousin, too?

HORACE: No. I'm kin to her on my father's side. She was my father's niece.

GORDON: Did she used to live here, too?

HORACE: Yes. A long time ago now.

GORDON: I thought I was kin to a lot of people. I thought I had a lot of cousins, but I said to Mama the other night: "I believe Cousin Horace is kin to a whole lot more. Why, if all of Cousin Horace's cousins traded with him in his store he would have the biggest business in south Texas." A lot of our cousins go to Houston, too. I said to Mama: "I don't understand it. Cousins going to Houston to trade, when their own cousin . . ."

HORACE (*interrupting*): I don't worry about it.

GORDON: You prefer the colored trade, don't you?

HORACE: Yes, I do.

GORDON: Why?

HORACE: I just do.

GORDON: I said to Mama: "Cousin Horace likes the colored trade." Brother heard me and he says: "White people won't go in his store on Saturday because of all the colored trade." "Cousin Horace doesn't care about that, Brother," I says.

(LEWIS HIGGINS *comes in. He is very drunk.*)

Hello, Cousin Lewis.

(LEWIS *doesn't answer. He stands facing the men for a minute.*)

LEWIS (*mumbling angrily*): Don't give me any shit! I don't have to take any shit!

(*There is silence.* HORACE *hums a bar or two of "After the Ball."*)

GORDON: These showers are bad for the cotton, Cousin Lewis, don't you think? (*Pause.*) How's your cotton crop? (*Pause.*)

LEWIS: Don't give me any shit! I don't have to take any shit! Not from anybody!

(*There is another pause.* HORACE *again hums a few bars of "After the Ball."* LEWIS *turns and leaves.*)

GORDON: Cousin Lewis is drunk. Someone ought to call Cousin Lester to come and get him and take him home. Cousin Lester doesn't drink at all, no, but he don't pay his bills, Brother says, and he owes everybody in town. Brother is bitter because they ended up with land that Mama says belonged to us. That was stolen from our grandfather. Yours too, Cousin Horace. Are you bitter about it? Brother says they own near two thousand acres that should have been at least half ours. How did it happen they wound up with it? Did you ever get it straight?

HORACE: No. And I don't lose any sleep over it and I advise you not to.

GORDON: I know, I heard you say that before and I told Brother you said that and he said: "Oh, well, it's just fine for Cousin Horace to talk that way, he's married to a wife who has a daddy and he'll inherit land one day. You and me have nothing." "We have a farm, Brother," I said, "that Mr. Henry Vaughn insisted Mama pay out when Daddy died instead of turning back to him." "A hundred acres, you call that a farm?" he says. "Only a fourth of it worth putting in cotton. The rest overrun with Johnson grass." (*Pause.*) Mama says your mama has had the worst time of all. She says she's had a hard time being a widow and all and having two boys to raise, but she says your mama has had to work the hardest of all and she has very poor health. She says she could have used the money for the land that was stolen from our grandfather. She told Cousin Lily Dale that one day and I said Cousin Horace said he didn't worry about it. And Cousin Lily Dale said Cousin Horace is a stick-in-the-mud and doesn't worry about anything. She said that she got a letter from a man in England who said he had found out there was a great estate over there that belonged to the Robedauxs. And he was asking all the Robedaux heirs in America to put up a hundred dollars each so he could go to court and get hold of the estate for them, since it was now worth millions. And she said you refused to pay out even a hundred dollars, and that Cousin Monty Reeves came to you and asked you to put five hundred dollars in an oil pool that he practically guaranteed and that you wouldn't do it and that the oil pool has brought thousands of dollars to all its investors and here you are still running a country store not half making it. "He does well," I said, "Cousin Lily Dale, when we have a cotton crop." "Cotton is through," Cousin Will said. "It's through, but he is so behind the time he doesn't know it." "Daddy . . . ," that's what Cousin Lily Dale calls Cousin Will now all the time since they have had the baby. "Daddy says Brother will never have a dime of his own, because he has no foresight. And he refuses to take chances." "I don't refuse to take chances," Cousin Will said. "No, you certainly don't," Cousin Lily Dale said. And then Cousin Will just laughed like he had heard the funniest thing in the world and he said: "I am now buying my second home, a two-story brick, in one of the nicest Houston suburbs and I am planning to be the richest man in Houston some day." "And he will be, too," Cousin Lily Dale said. And Aunt Corella and Cousin Pete both said they thought he would too, because there was no stopping him once he sets his mind to anything. And Mama agreed with them, too. "Well, Mama," I said later, after they had all gone back to Houston, "Cousin Horace has responsibilities. He has a wife and two children to support. And bills to pay to keep his store running, and suppose he had lost the five hundred dollars. What then?" "Well, he wouldn't have lost it," she said. "He would have made millions by now." "But he didn't know that, Mama." I said. "That's why he took the five hundred dollars instead and bought the rent house from Mr. Vaughn." "A rent house that is so rundown," she said, "that only trash will live in it. And who he can never get to pay their rent." "That may be," I said, "but he owns it and he didn't lose it and he could have lost five hundred dollars in an oil pool." But you can't argue with Mama as far as Cousin Lily Dale and Cousin Will are concerned. She thinks the sun rises and sets in Cousin Will. He bought Cousin Lily Dale a new car, you know. A Packard. He has a Packard and she has a Packard. Imagine, two Packards by the time you're thirty-seven! (*Pause.*) Do you think you'll ever get a car, Cousin Horace?

HORACE: What do I need a car for? I've got legs. I like to walk.

GORDON: Well, a car is nice to take you out to the farms.

HORACE: I don't have any farms.

GORDON: Well, to get you into Houston.

HORACE: I can take a train to Houston.

(LEWIS *comes back in.*)

GORDON: Hello, there, Cousin Lewis.

LEWIS: Who are you?

GORDON: Cousin Gordon.

LEWIS: Cousin Gordon who?

GORDON: Cousin Gordon Kirby, Cousin Lewis. This is your cousin Horace.

(LEWIS *looks at* HORACE *and then back at* GORDON.)

LEWIS: You're no cousin of mine, you ugly sonovabitch.

GORDON: Sure I am, Cousin Lewis. Your mama and my mama . . . (*Pause.*) How is it we're kin, Cousin Horace?

HORACE: I don't remember. (*Walks away.*)

GORDON: Sure you do. You just . . .

HORACE: No. I don't remember at all. (*Goes off.*)

GORDON: Don't let him hurt your feelings, Cousin Lewis. He can be awfully gruff sometimes, but he doesn't mean anything by it. He gets to worrying over his business. He had to borrow a little money from the bank last week to pay some invoices and that always worries him. He has only taken in two dollars all today, $1.98 to be exact. For a pair of overalls. Of course, nobody else in town is doing any better, you know. Nobody on the streets. Stores all empty; it's the rain. That worries Cousin Horace. "What if they have a run of bad, wet years," he said, like they had when he was a boy? And they have six or seven years of crop failures? What happens then? Of course, he didn't say that to me, but I overheard him talking to Mr. Douglas. Mr. Douglas said they would all have to close up is all, except those that had something in reserve. Mr. Douglas said the good times during the war fooled a lot of people into thinking high prices and good times and plentiful money would be forever.

LEWIS: Are you Brother Vaughn?

GORDON: No. I'm not Brother Vaughn. I'm your cousin . . . Gordon Kirby. Brother Vaughn used to work in here. He's not kin to you though; Horace is kin to you. Brother Vaughn is his brother-in-law.

LEWIS: Where is Brother Vaughn?

GORDON: He's gone back on a boat. This time he's gone to Germany.

LEWIS: He's a good old boy. He testified for me at my trial.

GORDON: That's right, he did. He sure did. I remember that.

LEWIS: He knows how to drink.

GORDON: Yes, I guess he does. I'm having a dance again in two weeks, Cousin Lewis . . .

LEWIS: Have you got a drink on you?

GORDON: No, I sure don't.

LEWIS: You don't drink?

GORDON: No Sir. I don't.

LEWIS: A sonovabitch that don't drink isn't worth killing.

GORDON: No Sir.

LEWIS: Whose boy are you?

GORDON: I'm Cousin Inez's boy.

LEWIS: Who is Cousin Inez?

GORDON: Your cousin. You know . . .

LEWIS: Where's she live?

GORDON: Right here. Same as you. Born and raised here.

HORACE (*coming back*): I'm going for a cup of coffee. I'll be right back.

GORDON: Yes Sir.

(HORACE *goes.*)

LEWIS: Who is that?

GORDON: That's my cousin Horace. He's your cousin, too.

LEWIS: Did you ever know an old boy named Jamie Dale?

GORDON: Yes Sir.

LEWIS: Well, he's a cousin of mine somewhere down the line. I called him cousin, too. Cuz, that is. Was he a cousin of yours?

GORDON: No Sir.

LEWIS: Well, you said you were a cousin of mine.

GORDON: Yes Sir. I am, too. But he wasn't my cousin.

LEWIS: Well, he was mine.

GORDON: Yes Sir.

LEWIS: But I said to him: "Look a here . . . I don't allow you to speak to women that way in my presence, cousin or no. I wasn't raised that way and I don't think you were, no matter how drunk you are. I don't care how drunk I am or how drunk you are, or how drunk they are. I can't permit it." You see, he was calling them whores. He was saying they was both whores, and they resented it, naturally, and I said: "I told you once, Jamie. I don't want you speaking that way to ladies in my presence." But he went on saying "whore this and whore that" . . . just a lot of dirty words, you know. And I said: "Now listen here, we weren't raised that way to talk that way in front of ladies, so shut up!" "I'll shut you up!" he says. And he drew a knife and started for me and I says: "No you don't." And I drew my knife and that's when I cut him. If I hadn't, he'd a killed me. You ask the ladies that was with us. They both testified as to how it was.

(ELIZABETH ROBEDAUX *comes in.*)

ELIZABETH: Hello, Lewis. Hello, Gordon.

GORDON: Hello, Cousin Elizabeth. Cousin Horace just went for a cup of coffee.

ELIZABETH: Did he go to the drugstore or the restaurant?

GORDON: He didn't say.

ELIZABETH: I'll look in both places. In case I miss him, tell him to wait here until I come back.

GORDON: Yes Ma'am.

(*She goes.*)

LEWIS: Who is that lady?

GORDON: That's Cousin Elizabeth. She's married to Cousin Horace. We're kin to her by marriage.

LEWIS: We are? What's her name?

GORDON: Elizabeth. Elizabeth Robedaux. She was a Vaughn.

LEWIS: Is she kin to Brother Vaughn?

GORDON: They're brother and sister.

LEWIS: Brother Vaughn is her brother?

GORDON: Sure.

LEWIS: Why didn't you tell me that? Why in the world didn't you tell me that?

GORDON: I thought you knew it.

LEWIS: I think the world of Brother Vaughn. He's one good old boy. He can sure drink.

GORDON: Yes, he can.

(HORACE *comes in.*)

You just missed your wife.

HORACE: I did? Where did she go?

GORDON: She went looking for you. I told her you were having some coffee.

HORACE: I went to the post office after that.

GORDON: She said to wait here for her. That she would be right back here if she didn't catch you in the drugstore.

HORACE: All right.

LEWIS: Do you know old Brother Vaughn?

GORDON: Why, sure he does, Cousin Lewis. Cousin Horace is his brother-in-law.

LEWIS: Brother Vaughn is your cousin?

GORDON: No. No. Cousin Horace is my cousin. Your cousin, too. Brother Vaughn is his brother-in-law.

LEWIS: Oh, yes. As soon as Brother Vaughn heard about my trouble he came over to the house and he says, "I'm going to stand by you. You're a good old boy and we were raised together and I want you to know you can count on me." "I want you to know exactly how it was," I said. "For we were raised together and no matter how sorry we act, how drunk we get, we do not allow a man to cuss a woman in our presence." "No, we do not," he says. Brother Vaughn says, "I would have done the same thing in your place. I would have cut the sonovabitch the same as you did and I want you to know that I am going to stand by you. You can count on me." (*Pause.*) Where is Brother Vaughn?

GORDON: He's in Germany. Cousin Horace?

HORACE: What?

GORDON: Isn't Brother Vaughn in Germany?

HORACE: Not quite yet. He's still on high seas. I think he arrives in Germany next week sometime.

LEWIS: Mr. Vaughn sent that sonovabitch over to Germany to make a man of him. That's what Brother Vaughn told me with his own mouth. "They are sending me to Germany to make a man of me. They think I drink too much whiskey, have the wrong friends. I know you," Brother Vaughn says. "And I know how you were raised. Just the same as me and we don't allow a man to cuss a woman in our presence. No matter what kind of woman they might be." Now, it is true, the kind of woman Jamie Dale and I were out with that night was not the kind of woman I would have cared to introduce to my mother had she been living, which she is not, since she died when I was three. And I never knew her at all to speak of . . . Still, I revere her memory and I respect her as I respect all women and that's why when Cousin Jamie started cursing these two women we was with . . . now, mind you we were all drunk and I allow for that. I want you to know I took it into allowance. But still and all, after I had warned him and asked as nice as I could: "Please, Jamie, do not use language like that to ladies in my presence. I ain't been raised that way and neither have you been," still . . .

ELIZABETH (*coming in*): Here you are.

HORACE: Everything all right with the children?

ELIZABETH: Yes.

HORACE: I was worried.

ELIZABETH: It's your mother. They called from Houston.

HORACE: Who did?

ELIZABETH: Your sister. Your mother has to be operated on again. They have taken her to the hospital.

HORACE: Is it serious?

ELIZABETH: I'm afraid so. I said we would take the train out in the morning. We will spend the night and be with your mother Monday morning when she is operated on.

HORACE: All right.

GORDON: Aunt Corella sick again?

HORACE: Yes. She's to have another operation. You will have to run the store for me Monday morning.

LEWIS: Who is Aunt Corella?

GORDON: His mother. She's your cousin. Cousin Corella, you call her.

LEWIS: Cousin Corella?

GORDON: She was a Thornton, then she married a Robedaux who is Cousin Horace's father. Then he died and now she is married to Mr. Davenport and I call him Cousin Pete. But he's not really my cousin. He's my uncle by marriage. And Cousin Horace calls him Mr. Davenport although he's his stepdaddy.

LEWIS: My mama died, you know, when I was three. She had it fixed so my daddy couldn't get hold of her inheritance. It came directly to me and my brother. My granddaddy said he gets the credit for fixing it that way. No matter how many wives and children my daddy had he couldn't give our land to them or divide it amongst them. Brother says that hurt Daddy so, when he found out how Mama had made out her will, that he just gave up and died, too. Granddaddy says it wasn't so. He says my daddy wasn't much to start with and if he had ever gotten his hands on what my brother and I had we would have wound up with nothing. As it is, I've got a thousand acres of fine cotton land and so has my brother. But like Brother Vaughn says, a loss of a mother is a terrible thing. I know one night we were all on our way to Houston, drunk, and we stopped by Richmond on the way there and we went out to this bootlegger we knew about in the country to get us some whiskey and when we went inside there was strangers there and we didn't know a soul, not a living soul . . . except for one man who reminded me later he was my cousin. My fifth cousin, I think he said. And Brother Vaughn can talk, you know, when he has a mind to, and he says to all those people there: "Good people . . . good people. You don't know us and we don't know you. But here is an old boy before you that lost his mother when he was three. And that's a sad, terrible thing. Now, I have a mother and I trust the rest of you have, this old boy doesn't." Well, I tell you those men couldn't do enough for me. They all felt so bad, they said, about my mother dying. They all had to buy me a drink of whiskey and Brother Vaughn a drink of whiskey because he was my good friend. Well, Sir, they bought us so much whiskey and we got so drunk we never did get to Houston. We just spent the whole day and night out in the country in Richmond drinking whiskey until we both passed out and some good, kind person put us to bed. Anyway, that's the kind of friend Brother Vaughn was.

(HENRY VAUGHN *comes in.*)

MR. VAUGHN: Horace, you really should have a phone in this store. They've called again from Houston. Your mother may not have an operation, she's so very low. They want you in Houston at once.

HORACE: There's no train to Houston until in the morning.

MR. VAUGHN: I'm going to drive you and Elizabeth in.

HORACE: Yes Sir.

(*He turns to* GORDON.)

Gordon . . . Did you hear that?

GORDON: Yes Sir.

HORACE: You'll have to close the store by yourself.

GORDON: Yes Sir. How late tonight do you want me to stay open?

HORACE: Well, if it stays as quiet as this, you can close around nine-thirty or ten.

GORDON: Yes Sir.

MR. VAUGHN: Your mama has gone over to be with the children, Elizabeth.

ELIZABETH: Yes Sir.

(HORACE *has gone to the back of the store.*)

Who called?

MR. VAUGHN: Your mama answered the phone. She said it was Lily Dale but she was upset. She couldn't talk and she had to put her husband on the phone.

(HORACE *comes back to them with his hat.*)

HORACE: Let's go.

(*They start out.*)

I'll call you tomorrow, Gordon.

GORDON: Yes Sir.

(HORACE, ELIZABETH, *and* MR. VAUGHN *leave.*)

LEWIS: Who was that gentleman?

GORDON: That's Cousin Horace. He owns this store.

LEWIS: Does he own the building, too?

GORDON: No. His cousin Jackson Hindell owns the building. He has law offices upstairs. Cousin Horace rents it from Cousin Jackson. But he owns all the stock. At least I think it's all paid for. He had to borrow a little from the bank to pay out his last invoice. I don't know how much, though. I do know it worried him. He's a hard worker, you know. But then times are tight. Not like during the war when everybody was making money.

LEWIS: And who was the other man? Is he a cousin, too?

GORDON: No. That's Brother Vaughn's papa. Mr. Henry Vaughn.

LEWIS: Of course, it was Mr. Henry Vaughn. Where are my manners? Why didn't you tell me so I could have spoken to him? I know his boy, you know, Brother Vaughn. We were raised up together.

GORDON: I know him, too, Cousin Lewis. I was born and raised here the same as you were.

LEWIS: And what's your name?

GORDON: Cousin Gordon. I'm Cousin Inez's son. You know.

LEWIS: Oh, yes. I'm going to find Mr. Henry Vaughn and I'm going to apologize to him for not knowing who he was right away and speaking to him. I don't want Mr. Henry Vaughn to think I've forgotten all manners. (*Wanders out.*)

(*The lights fade.*)

(*The lights come up on a hospital waiting room. It's early evening of the same day.* WILL KIDDER *is reading the afternoon paper.* MONTY REEVES *enters with his wife,* LOLA. *They are both dressed in expensive clothes and* LOLA *wears lots of jewelry.*)

MONTY: Hello, Cousin Will.

WILL: Hello, Cousin Monty. Hello, Cousin Lola.

LOLA: Hello, Cousin Will. (*Pause.*) Well, we're mighty sorry.

MONTY: How is Cousin Corella?

WILL: You know, it's very serious. But we are not giving up hope, you know.

LOLA: Of course you can't give up hope. You can't ever do that.

MONTY: It's all in God's hands, Cousin Will.

WILL: Oh, I believe that. I'm not a very good Christian, you know. I mean my record of church attendance could be greatly improved, but I do believe it is all in God's hands.

LOLA: And He knows best, Cousin Will. We can't ever question whatever he sends, no matter how hard it seems. Where is Cousin Lily Dale?

WILL: She's with her mama.

LOLA: Worried to death, I know. Bless her heart, worried to death. Oh, they are so close as mother and daughter, just inseparable. I said to Monty, I said: "Monty, what will happen to Lily Dale if anything happens to her mama?" Why, they are on the phone to each other the first thing every morning. Why, once when I was in Houston visiting Cousin Corella, the phone rang at seven in the morning. And I said: "Who can that be calling you at this hour?" She was up, of course, because she gets up, as you know, every morning at five to fix Cousin Pete's breakfast. "Why, it's Lily Dale," she said, "she calls me every morning or I call her every morning by seven. If she didn't call me by then, I'd be worried to death." Isn't that devotion? "And we try to see each other every day," she said, "and we always talk on the phone at least five times before bedtime." Isn't that devotion? I wish my sweet mama and I were devoted like that. But we aren't. Mama is very opinionated.

MONTY: And I suppose you aren't?

LOLA: Yes, I am opinionated, but not like Mama. No one in this world was ever born as opinionated as Mama.

WILL: How did you all hear about Miss Corella?

LOLA: Well, it's strange. We've taken an apartment at the Plaza which we keep the year round although we don't live in Houston the year round. Monty, you know, is prospering because of this oil lease he had the foresight . . .

MONTY (*interrupting*): I did everything in the world except take a pistol to him to get Cousin Horace to come in on it, you know.

WILL: Shoot, I know. You can't do anything with Horace. He's a mossback.

LOLA: That's exactly what Monty said to him. We're not talking behind his back, he said it right to his face: "Cousin Horace, you're a mossback."

WILL: I'm doing pretty well, too, you know. My business is just wonderful. Just bought my second home. I wish you had come to me about that oil lease.

MONTY: I wish I had, too, Cousin Will.

WILL: Remember me the next time.

MONTY: Yes, indeed.

LOLA: Anyway, we were in the lobby at the Plaza when Mae Buchaman came in and said she had sent the overseer of her farm to go into Cousin Horace's and line up some Christmas presents for her tenants. She said she buys a handkerchief or a shirt or pants for each of her tenants from Cousin Horace every year, as he knows all the tenants and their sizes, and she does it early every year, or gets her overseer to, because by October she's heading for Europe. Isn't that the life? Inherited wealth, too, you know. Every penny of it, never made a dime herself and it's a wonder she has any of it left the kind of no-good men she's always married. But she has money still, enough to buy and sell all of us. Anyway, she said her overseer called to say that Cousin Horace wasn't in the store.

MONTY: I don't think she's kin to Horace, is she?

LOLA: Who?

MONTY: Mae Buchaman.

LOLA: Oh, I think she is. I mean maybe distant. But I

think they're kin. Aren't they, Will? Aren't Lily Dale and Horace and all of them kin to Mae Buchaman?

WILL: I swear, I don't know. I can't keep all the kin straight.

MONTY: I know I'm sure as hell not.

LOLA: Well, you may not be. But Horace and Lily Dale are kin to a lot of people you aren't kin to. Just like you are kin to a lot of people they aren't. I mean we can't all be kin to the same people.

MONTY: You may be right.

LOLA: I know I'm right.

MONTY: Did she call him Cousin Horace?

LOLA: No. But everybody doesn't call their cousins cousins.

MONTY: You said she did.

LOLA: I did not.

MONTY: You did too. You said the overseer said Cousin Horace was not in the store and . . .

LOLA (*interrupting*): That's what I call him. I didn't say she called him that. I don't remember what she called him, but I bet she wouldn't call him that even if they were first cousins. Why, she doesn't even call her mama Mama.

MONTY: What does she call her?

LOLA: Cassie Sue.

MONTY: Why does she call her Cassie Sue?

LOLA: Because that is her Christian name. (*Laughs.*) I'd

like to see Mama's expression if I started calling her by her Christian name of Sally Grace. She'd slap me across the mouth. Anyway, the overseer told Mae that Horace had left the store in charge of Cousin Gordon and was heading for Houston because his mama was near death's door at the hospital. "What hospital, Mae?" I asked. But she didn't know that and I said, "Well, Monty, there's only one thing to do. Call every hospital in the city of Houston until we find where she is." And we did. What time is Cousin Horace going to get here?

WILL: I don't know. They're driving.

LOLA: How's Cousin Pete?

WILL: Half crazy.

LOLA: It's a terrible expense, isn't it?

WILL: It's awful.

LOLA: How many operations has she had?

WILL: Three.

LOLA: My God! And all of them serious?

WILL: Two of them were.

LOLA: What is it, honey?

WILL: They don't know. She doesn't feel well half the time. Her blood pressure is just terrible. It's so high and her heart isn't too good.

LOLA: Oh, poor thing.

WILL: But they hope that this one last operation will fix her up, if they can operate. At first the doctors didn't know.

But they decided to go ahead in the morning. She's not herself half the time, you know. They have her all doped up. The only person she seems to keep straight is Lily Dale. Pete went in to see her before he had to go to work and he says he doesn't think she knew at all who he was.

LOLA: My goodness!

WILL: She looks just whipped down to me, to tell you the truth.

LOLA: She's worked like a dog all her life, Will. You and I know that. I saw Minnie Curtis uptown the other day at Munn's and she was going on about all those things that happened when Cousin Corella was married to her first husband, and what she had to say about Cousin Corella, frankly, wasn't too nice. I said: "Minnie, I don't care to hear all of that."

MONTY: Do you think if we stop back by in half an hour or so, we could see Cousin Horace?

WILL: He might be here by then.

LOLA: Why don't we come back then? Now, we both want you to know you can call on us day and night for anything.

WILL: Thank you.

(LOLA *and* MONTY *leave.* WILL *goes back to his paper.* PETE DAVENPORT *comes in.*)

PETE: I saw Monty in the hall. What's the name of his wife?

WILL: Lola.

PETE: Oh, yes. They said they would be back later. Any change?

WILL: No. Lily Dale came out about an hour ago. She said she was sleeping.

PETE: The doctor with her?

WILL: No.

PETE: Do you think I can go in?

WILL: I don't see why not.

(PETE *goes out.* WILL *goes back to his paper.* MR. VAUGHN, ELIZABETH, *and* HORACE *enter.*)

Come in, folks. Come in.

(*He extends his hand to* HORACE.)

How are you, young man?

HORACE: All right, Will. Thank you.

WILL: How are you, Elizabeth?

ELIZABETH: Hello, Will. Will, this is my father.

WILL: How do you do, Sir. It's a great pleasure. I'm honored to meet such a successful man. How was the trip?

ELIZABETH: It was tiring. The roads are so bad because of the rain.

WILL: Well, that's what you get for living out in the sticks. I was raised in the country you know, know all about it.

HORACE: How is Mama?

WILL: I don't know, fellow. We're all worn out from it, let me tell you. Well, you know how your mama is, she never complains about anything. I mean she's always thinking of somebody else and doing for them. Why, you know when Lily Dale had the baby, of course she had a terrible time and she's never been strong in the first place. Why, your mama just moved right over a month before the baby was expected and she didn't leave her side hardly, day or night, until that baby of ours was born, and he is a cute little fellow, let me tell you. We took him over to my first cousin's house, Wilma Maud. Do you know her, Horace?

HORACE: No. I don't think I do.

WILL: Well, we took him over there because Lily Dale was half crazy worrying over your mama and I didn't know in what way I might be needed. So Cousin Wilma Maud said she would be happy to have him. I said, "Of course you would. It's a privilege to take care of a kid like that." I never have seen a smarter four-year-old in my life. I mean he can play baseball better than I can right now and he just goes up to that new piano I bought Lily Dale . . . Of course, you haven't seen the new piano I bought Mud.

HORACE: Who is Mud?

WILL: That's what I call Lily Dale now that she's a mother. She calls me Daddy and I call her Mud. Guess what I paid for the piano? (*Pause.*) What do you think that set me back? A thousand bucks. The best they had. A thousand dollars. "Will," Lily said: "Can we afford that, Daddy?" "Of course, we can afford it," I told her, "I only want the best in this house of ours. We are going to spare no expense." The best piano, the best rugs, the best living-room furniture, the best dining room set, the best bed-room suite. We have them all. I bought all this, a new house, and two Packards all in the same year. Not bad, is it, for an old boy from East Texas who came to Houston not more than twelve years ago without a nickel in my pocket? You know what they say about you, Mr. Vaughn? They say you have the Midas touch. They say everything you touch turns to gold. Well, now, I must have been kin to you somewhere down the road, somewhere back there we're cousins, I bet. Because I have the Midas touch. Everything I touch makes money. Shoot, like I told Lily Dale, it better had, the way we're spending it.

HORACE: You were telling me about Mama.

WILL: Oh, yes. I certainly was. Let's see. How much do you know?

HORACE: You called the house around noon and told Elizabeth we should come over on Sunday and then you called back and told Mr. Vaughn we'd better get right here as soon as we could.

WILL: That's right. We certainly did. Well, your mama and Pete were spending the night with us night before last. They are so crazy about the baby they are always begging us to go out so they can take care of it. So Mud and I decided to go out to dinner and they came over and when Lily Dale came home, the first thing she said to your mama is, "You don't look well." And your mama said: "To tell you the absolute truth, I don't feel well." Now between Lily Dale and your mama, they know every doctor in Houston, and as you know, your mama wasn't at all satisfied with her last two operations and Lily Dale has had two herself, not counting the Caesarean for the baby. And Lily Dale said, "I tell you what, this time we're going to get you to a good doctor." And they began to talk over the pros and cons of the doctors they knew and finally decided on one, Dr. Keith Edwards. And Lily Dale called him and she said it was an emergency and he was to come over right away. Well, he got here and he examined her and he said she was a very sick woman and she would have to undergo a major operation on Monday and that it was serious. And they'd better get her to the hospital right away. And we took her right over and we came back here and called your house to tell you, and Lily Dale was getting some things ready to take to your mama in the hospital when they called us from there and they said she was much worse and they weren't sure they could operate and to get over there as soon as we could. So we put in another call to you all and came on over here. We've been here ever since.

ELIZABETH: What's wrong with her, Will? Did they say?

WILL: No. They're not sure yet. She's very sick. That's all they say. Your Cousin Monty and your Cousin Lola were here. They said they were coming by later to speak to you. Are they your first or second cousins?

HORACE: Second. Can I see Mama?

WILL: Lily Dale and Mr. Davenport are in there now.

HORACE: Maybe I'd better wait then.

WILL: No. I'll tell them you're here. Cousin Gordon called, by the way, Horace, he wanted you to call him as soon as you got here.

HORACE: Did he say what it was about?

WILL: No. There's a phone out in the hall. He said to call him at the store. I said, "Will you still be at the store when he gets here?" He said he thought he would be.

HORACE: I don't have a phone at the store.

WILL: Don't you?

HORACE: No.

ELIZABETH: Call next door at Douglas's. They'll call him to their phone.

WILL: Come on. I'll show you where the phone is.

(*He goes out and* HORACE *follows after him.*)

ELIZABETH: Papa, I don't want you to go back over those roads tonight.

MR. VAUGHN: We'll see.

ELIZABETH: You can stay with Aunt Eva tonight. Call Mama and tell her.

MR. VAUGHN: I'll see.

ELIZABETH: I know Mama would want you to stay.

MR. VAUGHN: We'll see.

(WILL *comes in.*)

WILL: There has been a robbery of some sort at the store.

ELIZABETH: Oh, my goodness!

WILL: I couldn't catch everything he said, but I gathered that much.

ELIZABETH: That's too bad.

WILL: I'd never leave any business of mine in charge of Cousin Gordon. He means well, I'm sure.

ELIZABETH: There was nothing else he could do under the circumstances.

WILL: I guess.

HORACE (*coming in*): There were two drawers of shirts stolen, Gordon said. He was in the back showing a customer some work clothes when these two men opened the two shirt drawers in the front showcase right quick and ran out before he had time to even holler at them to stop. Of course, that's his story. I bet he was in the back taking a nap.

ELIZABETH: Twice after Horace came home for dinner he found him sitting up sound asleep in a chair in the back of the store. He said the whole town could have come in and walked off with everything he had in the store and poor Gordon was so sound asleep he would have never known it.

HORACE: Of course, he promised both times it would never happen again.

WILL: I'd get me a new clerk.

HORACE: I feel sorry for him. His mother is a widow, you know, and he's trying to get an education.

PETE (*coming in*): Hello, Horace. Hello, Elizabeth.

ELIZABETH: Do you know my father, Mr. Davenport?

PETE: How do you do.

WILL: Can Horace go in?

PETE: I don't know what to say. She's a very sick woman. I don't think I better say. You had better ask Lily Dale.

WILL: I'll ask her. (*Goes.*)

PETE: How was the ride over?

ELIZABETH: It took over four hours. We left around one.

PETE: The roads bad?

ELIZABETH: Terrible.

PETE: They'll have that road paved one day.

HORACE: I hope I have a store left when I get back.

ELIZABETH: I'm sure he'll be extra careful now. Did he call the sheriff?

HORACE: Yes, he did. He said he took down all the information.

ELIZABETH: Horace had some shirts stolen out of his store.

PETE: What do you get for shirts?

HORACE: Depends on the quality of the shirt. Start at ninety-five cents, then I've got some for a dollar twenty-five and some for a dollar fifty and then a dollar ninety-five, for the best ones.

PETE: What do you think I paid for this?

HORACE (*feeling Mr. Davenport's shirt*): I don't know.

PETE: Sixty-five cents. I wouldn't pay more for a shirt. There is a store here in Houston I go to that undersells everybody. How is your business?

HORACE: A little slow now.

WILL (*coming in*): Lily Dale says come ahead, but not to stay long.

HORACE: Where do I go?

WILL: Come on. I'll take you.

(*They leave as the lights fade. The lights are brought up on another part of the stage on a small hospital room.* CORELLA DAVENPORT *is in bed.* LILY DALE KIDDER *sits beside her.* CORELLA *has her eyes closed. She opens them.*)

CORELLA: What did Will want?

LILY DALE: He said Brother is here. He's coming in now to see you.

(*Pause.*)

CORELLA: Do I look all right?

LILY DALE: You look fine. Don't worry about it. You know Brother is not going to pay any attention to how you look.

(HORACE *comes to the edge of the room.*)

Come on in, Brother.

(HORACE *comes slowly into the room and goes over to the bed.*)

CORELLA: Hello, Son. I'm sorry you had to come in like this on a Saturday. I know that's your busy day.

HORACE: It wasn't all that busy. How do you feel?

CORELLA: Oh, I don't feel so good. I don't like to complain, but I don't feel at all good. The doctor says I've just worn myself out. But he said no wonder when I told him how I had to work as a young woman. All the meals I cooked for those boarders. And he said, "You want to live, don't you?"

LILY DALE: And do you know what she said, Brother? She said she wasn't sure if she did or not and I said, "She does, too, want to live. She has a wonderful grandchild."

CORELLA: And what did I say?

LILY DALE: What?

CORELLA: What did I say?

LILY DALE: Oh, what did you say?

CORELLA: I said I had three.

LILY DALE: Three what?

CORELLA: Grandchildren. You said I wanted to live because I had one grandchild and I said I had three.

LILY DALE: Oh, I meant you had one grandchild here in Houston.

CORELLA: But I have three in all.

LILY DALE: I know that, Mama.

CORELLA: How are your children, Son?

HORACE: They're fine, Mama.

CORELLA: And Elizabeth?

HORACE: She's fine. She came with me.

CORELLA: Did she? Who's taking care of the children?

HORACE: Mrs. Vaughn.

CORELLA: Lily Dale, you go get a little rest for yourself while Horace and I have a little visit.

LILY DALE: All right. (*Goes.*)

CORELLA: She's been so good to me. She watches over me day and night. She and Will insisted I take a single room. They had me in a double room at first, but the woman they had in the room with me talked so much I thought I would lose my mind. Have you been all right?

HORACE: Yes Ma'am.

CORELLA: You have quite a struggle, don't you, making a living for a wife and your two children? You've worked as hard as I have. Lily Dale doesn't like me to say that. She hasn't had the easiest time in the world, no one knows that better than me. But you've had the hardest time of all. I wish I could make it up to you some way. Sometimes I don't sleep at night for worry over what's happened or what might happen, but worry doesn't change anything. The doctor says I have to cut out worrying, he says worry is killing me. (*Pause.*) Do you worry, Son?

HORACE: Yes Ma'am, I do. Too much, I reckon.

CORELLA: Lily Dale doesn't worry. Will doesn't worry. He's doing very well, Son.

HORACE: Is he?

CORELLA: Built them a perfectly beautiful new house. Got a baby grand piano and furnished the whole house beautifully. I hate to think what it cost him. He bought two Packards, too. Did you know that? I wonder why we worry and he doesn't? I once said to him, I said: "Will, what's your secret? How do you keep from worrying? If you could teach me that, I'd be the happiest woman in the world." Will said you can't teach something like that. You're born with it. (*Pause.*) I wanted to see you alone, to ask you if you had heard from your Cousin Minnie?

HORACE: No Ma'am. Not since she came out to look at Papa's and Uncle's tombstones.

CORELLA: Well, she said she was writing you. I ran into her at the ladies' room at Foley's and I tried to avoid her, but she cornered me. She was in a hurry. She went back over my marriage to your papa and I said: "Minnie, that's all past." "For you," she said, "but not for me. And Horace has never forgiven you for running off and leaving him." And I said: "Minnie, you are crazy. No one ever left anybody." "You did," she said. "You left your husband and you left your son." "I had to leave him," I said. "I simply couldn't stand what was going on another day." "What was going on you couldn't stand?" she said. "Why, if you don't know by now," I said, "I'm not going to tell you." "I don't know, because you don't know," she said. "Nothing went on but your meanness . . ." And then I lost my temper. God forgive me. And right there in Foley's ladies' room I began to holler and scream at your Cousin Minnie like a crazy woman. I said terrible things about your grandmother and your uncles, and your father. I said things I had long ago forgotten. And she said she would never forgive me for the things I said. And that she was going to tell you all about it and she bet you would never forgive me.

HORACE: She hasn't told me anything.

CORELLA: I think she's half crazy, Son. She goes over all that all the time, like it happened just yesterday, and I think that's driven your Cousin Minnie right out of her mind. (*Pause.*) I didn't tell Lily Dale any of this. I saw no sense in upsetting her.

HORACE: No Ma'am.

CORELLA: I'd like to spend the rest of my time here on earth at peace with everyone. I'll know better next time to even talk to your Cousin Minnie. If she tries to talk to me, I'll just go on about my business. I heard from your Cousin Lily Roberts that the rest of your cousins on your father's side are doing well. Carlton is studying to be a doctor. Lily Roberts has a son about your son's age. Another cousin, Raymond, I think, has a drugstore. (*Pause.*) Cousin Minnie said she despised me and that you hated me. She said when you were here at the business school and living in the same house with her that you would never have gotten through business school if it hadn't been for her helping you. She said she was the only one in your whole life that had ever taken any interest in you. (*Pause.*) Do you hate me, Son?

HORACE: No Ma'am. I don't hate you. You know that, Mama. Why do you ask something foolish like that?

CORELLA: And you never told Minnie you hated me? Did you?

HORACE: No Ma'am.

CORELLA: And did you tell her she was the only member of your family that ever took any interest in you?

HORACE: No Ma'am. I couldn't have. That wouldn't be true. My aunts have always been good to me and Aunt Inez certainly has been interested in everything I've ever done, and always tried to encourage me to get ahead. And Grandma and Grandpa did too, before they died.

CORELLA: And I was always interested. Of course we lived apart and circumstances were such that I . . . (*Pause.*) Did you see Pete?

HORACE: Yes Ma'am.

CORELLA: He's been so good to me, Son.

HORACE: Yes Ma'am.

CORELLA: And Lily Dale. And Will has treated me like he was my own son.

LILY DALE (*coming in*): What have you all been talking about?

CORELLA: Nothing. I've just been hearing all about his children.

LILY DALE: Cousin Monty and Cousin Lola are out there talking to Elizabeth. (*To* HORACE:) They've come by especially to say hello to you, they said.

HORACE: I'll go speak to them. (*Starts out.*)

LILY DALE (*to* HORACE): And Will says Cousin Minnie Curtis called asking to speak to you. He said he couldn't get you now and he said she wants you to call her back.

CORELLA: How did she know Horace was here?

LILY DALE: That's exactly what I asked Will. And Will says he asked her that same question. You know Will, he's not afraid of the devil; why, he'll ask anybody anything. Will said she ran into Mae Buchaman uptown shopping and she told her you were in the hospital and Horace had been sent for.

CORELLA: How did Mae Buchaman know I was here?

LILY DALE: God only knows. Do you know, Horace?

HORACE: No.

LILY DALE: Well, I'll say this . . . if she knows it, it won't be long before all of Houston will be told about it. She has the biggest mouth.

CORELLA: She's kin to us, you know.

LILY DALE: Mae Buchaman?

CORELLA: Yes.

LILY DALE: How?

CORELLA: I don't exactly remember, but she is, some way. We're cousins.

LILY DALE: On which side?

CORELLA: My side.

LILY DALE: I certainly never knew that. We don't call her cousin.

CORELLA: We don't call a lot of our cousins cousin.

LILY DALE: That's true enough. Horace, have you heard about my beautiful new house which Will has furnished so lavishly?

HORACE: Yes, I have.

LILY DALE: Who told you? Mama?

HORACE: No, Will.

LILY DALE: Did he? I bet he did. He's so proud of it. I want him to take you over there to spend the night so you can see everything. I have the most beautiful piano in the city of Houston and my drapes are the most expensive he could find. And the rugs, Horace . . .

HORACE: I think I'd better go and see Cousin Monty, Lily Dale. I don't want them to think I'm rude.

LILY DALE: All right.

(*He goes.* CORELLA *closes her eyes and then opens them.*)

CORELLA: How does Elizabeth seem?

LILY DALE: All right. Elizabeth is a disappointment to me, frankly, Mama.

CORELLA: How, honey?

LILY DALE: Well, I've never had a sister and when Brother married Elizabeth I thought at last I have a sister I can be close to. But I was in for a very bitter disappointment. I don't feel close to her at all. I find her really very cold, Mama.

CORELLA: Well, she has sisters of her own, Lily Dale.

LILY DALE: I know she does, but I don't and it looks like she could try in some way to be close to me. But all she thinks about, it seems to me, is Brother and her children. I must tell you, Mama, I find Elizabeth very self-centered.

CORELLA: I wonder what your Cousin Minnie wanted Horace for?

LILY DALE: God only knows.

CORELLA: Do you think he will call her?

LILY DALE: He might. He's always been close to Minnie, you know. I could never understand that. "Brother," I said, "as mean as she has talked about your mama, how can you have anything ever to do with her?" "Well, she helped me get through business school," he said. "I would never have made it without her."

CORELLA: I guess that's true, too. Do you think it is true?

LILY DALE: I don't know. I don't have any opinion at all about that, although I do wonder what good a two-month business course in Houston did him, when all he does is to run a men's store in a one-horse town.

CORELLA: Your brother doesn't look well, Sister. I think he looks worried.

LILY DALE: Well, I don't think he does at all. Why don't you ever worry about how I look? Why is it always Brother you worry about?

CORELLA: I worry about you, Lily Dale. You know that.

LILY DALE: It's news to me if you do. All I ever hear you worrying about is Brother. How poorly he looks, how hard he works having to support a wife and two children. As a matter of fact, I'm in very poor health myself, Mama. I have been delicate all my life. Any day now I may be needing another serious operation myself.

CORELLA: I know that, honey. I know that. Believe me. Oh, I worry about you and your health all the time, Lily Dale. Why, I'm hardly out of bed before I go to the phone to find out what kind of a rest you have had and when you were having your baby I thought I would lose my mind.

(LILY DALE *is crying*.)

Now, Lily Dale. Lily Dale . . .

LILY DALE: Elizabeth hurt my feelings.

CORELLA: How?

LILY DALE: She just bit my head off when I asked her a perfectly innocent question about Brother Vaughn. Why, she flew at me like a wasp.

CORELLA: Oh, I'm sure not. You're just sensitive, Lily Dale. Always have been.

(LILY DALE *wipes her eyes. There is silence. The lights fade and are brought up on the waiting room.* MONTY *and* LOLA *are there. They are drinking coffee.* WILL *and* ELIZABETH *are near them.* MR. VAUGHN *is in the corner with his eyes closed.* HORACE *comes in.* MONTY *gets up and goes to him.*)

MONTY: Well, Cousin Horace. I'm sorry we have to meet at times like this.

LOLA: How did Cousin Corella seem to you, Cousin Horace?

HORACE: She seemed pretty good.

LOLA: Did she know you?

HORACE: Yes, she did. Her mind is clear as a bell.

LOLA: Thank God for that. Is she awful weak?

HORACE: No. She doesn't seem to be.

MONTY: Did you tell her we were here?

HORACE: Yes, she knows you are here.

LOLA: We wanted to see her, you know, the worst way. But Will explained the doctor said only the closest of kin could go in. Her children, her husband, and Will.

MONTY: Well, Cousin Horace, I'm a rich man.

HORACE: I know you are.

MONTY: I sure don't mean to rub it in, but I wish you had taken my advice.

LOLA: Oh, it worries him so that you didn't. "Why, all of Cousin Horace's worries would be over by now if he had just listened to me and put in that five hundred dollars," Monty keeps saying. "Why, he'd be worth thousands now."

HORACE: Well, maybe there'll be another time.

MONTY: I hope so.

LOLA: Monty says this was the chance of a lifetime.

MONTY: You never hear of lightning striking twice, you know.

HORACE: I guess not.

LOLA: By the way, are you kin to Mae Buchaman?

HORACE: Yes.

LOLA: I thought so. Cousins?

HORACE: Yes.

LOLA: How?

HORACE: I'm not sure exactly. It's on my mother's side.

LOLA: On your mother's side?

HORACE: Yes.

LOLA: Well, then you're kin to her, too, Monty.

MONTY: No, I'm not. I'm not kin to her at all. No way.

LOLA: Well, if Cousin Horace is kin to her on Cousin Corella's side, then you're kin to her. Because you are kin to Cousin Corella.

MONTY: I can't help that. I'm not kin to Mae Buchaman. I never have been.

LOLA: I bet you are and just don't know it.

WILL: Did Lily Dale tell you your Cousin Minnie called?

HORACE: Yes.

WILL: She wanted you to call her back. She says she's at home.

HORACE: Thank you.

WILL: And Cousin Gordon called again. He asked you to call him as soon as you could. He's still at the store.

HORACE: Oh, my God! Did he say anything was wrong?

WILL: No, he didn't say anything.

(HORACE *goes.*)

MONTY: I'm not kin to Minnie Curtis, either. Thank God.

LOLA: I didn't say you were kin to her. Cousin Horace is kin to her on his father's side. But if he's kin to Mae Buchaman on your mother's side . . .

MONTY: I can't help it. I'm not kin to her. If I was kin to her I'd know it. Don't you think I'd know it? Don't you know everybody you're kin to?

LOLA: No. I bet I don't.

MONTY: Don't you know everybody you're kin to, Elizabeth?

ELIZABETH: No, I'm sure not.

MONTY: Well, I do.

LOLA: How can you know that?

MONTY: I just do know it.

WILL: You know what a fortuneteller told me the other day? I walked in her house and she took one look at my palm and she said: "I see money written all over your palm." She said: "You are going to be a millionaire in five years."

LOLA: I believe in fortunetellers. I go to them all the time.

WILL: I never went to one before. Lily Dale and I were taking a ride and Lily Dale says let's stop in here and get our fortunes told. And I said: "Shoot, Lily Dale, that's just a lot of foolishness." And she said: "Come on," and so to humor her I went and that's what she told me. And she told Lily Dale someone close to her was going to be sick very soon and now we're all here.

LOLA: Oh, I believe in them. What's the name of this one, Will? I do want to go to her.

WILL: Oh, I don't remember. You ask Lily Dale.

LOLA: Does she know her name?

WILL: Yes, she does.

LOLA: Good.

(HORACE *comes back in.*)

ELIZABETH: Everything all right?

HORACE: No. Gordon said Cousin Lewis Higgins came into the store after supper and he got mad at something Gordon said and he kicked in one side of the glass hat case. Cut his leg all up.

MONTY: Whose?

HORACE: Lewis's.

MONTY: My God!

HORACE: Had to take him to the hospital. Gordon says there is blood everyplace. But he says none of the hats were hurt.

LOLA: Is the hat case that big old case?

HORACE: Yes.

LOLA: That's expensive, too.

HORACE: Yes, it is.

LOLA: How will you get that fixed?

HORACE: I'll just have to buy some glass and pay someone to put it in.

LOLA: Will that be expensive?

HORACE: Yes, it will be.

LOLA: Will Cousin Lewis pay for it?

HORACE: Gordon said the police called his brother, Lester. And Gordon said he came by and told him not to worry about it; he would take care of the damage.

MONTY: He's a liar. He'll never pay for it. He owes every-body in town now. I bet he owes you money. Doesn't he?

HORACE: Fifteen dollars.

MONTY: Well, you're lucky it's not more. He owes some merchants two or three hundred dollars.

LOLA: Are they your cousins, too, Monty?

MONTY: Yes, they are. Both of them.

LOLA: Will, we have to leave. Please go ask Lily Dale the name of that fortuneteller before we leave.

WILL: All right.

MONTY: I'm going to no fortuneteller tonight.

LOLA: Nobody is asking you to go to any fortuneteller tonight.

MONTY: Well, just don't.

MR. VAUGHN (*opening his eyes*): Is Gordon your first clerk, Horace?

HORACE: Yes Sir. Except for Brother. Brother was a good salesman, I'll say that for him.

MR. VAUGHN: If you could keep him in the store. Brother's problem is he's restless. I bet he went crazy on that boat. I bet he couldn't wait to get off.

LOLA: Is he on a boat, Mr. Vaughn?

MR. VAUGHN: Yes Ma'am. He is working on a cotton boat. They sail for Germany.

LOLA: Isn't that wonderful?

MR. VAUGHN: I had a grocery store, you know. For many years. And I had a number of clerks in my time. Of course, a grocery store is a lot different than a dry-goods store. You can eat up all your profits in a grocery store. Friends used to say to me: "Henry, how do you keep your clerks from eating you out of house and home?" "Well," I said, "it's very simple. When I hire a new man I take him all around the store and I tell him to eat all he wants, at any time." And the first two days they all just would stuff themselves, but by the third day they were so sick of food, they didn't touch anything. (*Laughs.*)

(LILY DALE *and* WILL *come in.*)

LILY DALE: Horace, Mama wants to see you and Elizabeth.

HORACE: All right.

(HORACE *and* ELIZABETH *start out of the room.* LILY DALE *goes to* LOLA.)

LILY DALE: Oh, Lola, this fortuneteller is wonderful. Will told you what she said to him and about Mama, and do you know what she said to me? She said I was sensitive and in poor health, myself. And that I had a child.

LOLA: Did she really?

PETE (*coming in*): Where is Horace? Minnie Curtis is on the phone. She said she called once before and she asked him to call her back.

LILY DALE: He can't talk to her now. He's in with Mama. You go talk to her, Will. Tell her for heaven's sake to stop bothering Brother.

LOLA: She thinks your brother is crazy about her. She told me they were extremely close.

LILY DALE: He never sees her. He's not close to anybody but his wife and his children.

LOLA: He worships Elizabeth, doesn't he?

LILY DALE: I guess so. Though, if you ask me . . .

(WILL *pinches* LILY DALE *and motions toward* MR. VAUGHN,

who has his eyes closed again. LILY DALE *puts her hand over her mouth and gives a little giggle.* WILL *leaves.*)

You know what else the fortuneteller told me?

LOLA: What?

LILY DALE: That I was artistic. And that I shouldn't be tied down in a kitchen and keeping house. That I should be an artist.

LOLA: Oh, isn't that remarkable?

LILY DALE: And I just had to tell her how exactly right she was, and that I played the piano and I composed music both popular and classical, and she said she knew it all along. She said I didn't have to tell her anything. She said: "You prefer classical music to popular, don't you?" And I said: "Yes, how did you know?" She says: "It's all in your hand, honey. Just like money is all over your husband's hand." And I said: "Where?" And she said, "Right there."

(LILY DALE *traces a line in the palm of her hand.* LOLA *watches and then points to the line.*)

LOLA: Is that the one?

LILY DALE: That's the one.

LOLA: Isn't that remarkable? What's her name, honey?

LILY DALE: Madame Claire.

LOLA: Write this down, Monty.

(MONTY *does so.*)

What's the address?

LILY DALE: Post Oak.

LOLA: Where on Post Oak?

LILY DALE: I don't remember that. It's quite a way out from town, though.

(MONTY *writes it down as the lights fade. The lights are brought up on Corella's room as* ELIZABETH *and* HORACE *enter.*)

CORELLA: Did you call back your Cousin Minnie?

HORACE: No.

CORELLA: Are you going to call her while you're in Houston?

HORACE: No. I don't think so.

CORELLA: Maybe you had better call her. It might just make things worse if you don't. She'll blame me if you don't call her, and she's mad enough now at me as it is.

HORACE: I don't want to call her, Mama. Not tonight.

CORELLA: Will you call her tomorrow?

HORACE: Yes, I will.

CORELLA: You promise me?

HORACE: Yes, I do. I promise you.

CORELLA: And don't tell her I told you about our fuss. Even if she brings it up. You just listen like you never heard a word of it before.

HORACE: I will.

CORELLA: Minnie and I had a fuss, Elizabeth. About things that happened years ago and should all be forgotten.

(*She takes Elizabeth's hand.*)

Did you ever hear of such a family? I bet you don't carry on this way in your family.

ELIZABETH: Oh, yes, we do.

(CORELLA *turns her head away. She is crying.*)

CORELLA: Excuse me. I'm scared. I don't mean to cry, but I'm scared. Lily Dale goes all to pieces if I cry in front of her.

ELIZABETH: Cry all you want to.

CORELLA: It upsets Lily Dale to see me cry. It always has. I don't want to worry the poor little thing any more than I have to. She's had so much to worry her. She was telling me just now how worried she was that she was neglecting her music and her composing for her housework. Not that she doesn't love Will and her baby, she does. But she feels she is being forced to give up what she loves most in the world—her music—for cooking meals and making beds. Of course, once I'm strong and well again I can help out. I have my own housework done by nine in the morning, and what little cooking I do for Pete and myself I can have finished by nine-thirty, and so like I told her, when I'm well and strong, I can come over to her house and take over her housework and mind the baby, which is the greatest pleasure I have in life, while she is free to practice the piano and compose her music. "There's nothing in this world that can't be worked out," I told her, "if we're just patient enough." "I'm not patient, Mama," she said, "and that's my trouble. I want to be famous as a composer, and how can I ever find fame as a composer in Houston, Texas? I don't sleep anymore at nights worrying about it," she said. "I hate to hear that," I said, "Lily Dale, I know that Horace and I were born worriers, but I hoped you had been spared that." "You know nothing at all about me," she said, "You don't and Will doesn't." Well, I put it all down to nerves and worry about my operation.

(*She looks up at* ELIZABETH.)

You don't worry, do you?

ELIZABETH: Yes, I do.

CORELLA: I'm sorry to hear it. Will Kidder doesn't. He's never worried in his life, he says.

HORACE: That's what he says, Mama. I bet he worries.

CORELLA: You think so?

HORACE: Yes, indeed.

(CORELLA *closes her eyes.*) We'd better go. You look sleepy.

CORELLA: Don't go just yet. Stay with me just a second longer.

ELIZABETH: Did they give you something to make you drowsy?

CORELLA: Yes. They want me to have a good, long rest, they said. Because of the ordeal facing me in the morning. I said: "Don't give me any dope." I have a terrible fear of their giving me dope and turning me into a dope fiend like poor old Mrs. Claremore. That's what happened to her, you know. The doctors gave her morphine or something to quiet her while she was in the hospital and she turned into an addict. Do you remember her, Son?

HORACE: Yes, I do.

CORELLA: She sold everything she had to buy morphine. (*She cries again.*) I'm scared.

HORACE: Now, Mama.

CORELLA: "What's wrong with me?" I asked the doctor. "We're not sure," he said. "Then why are you operating on me?" I said, "if you're not sure." "To help us to find out," he said. "Find out what?" I said. "What's wrong with you," he said. (*Pause.*) Horace, have you spoken to the doctor?

HORACE: No Ma'am.

CORELLA: Please don't lie to me, Son, tell me the truth.

HORACE: That's the truth, Mama.

CORELLA: The doctor hasn't told Will and Lily Dale anything he hasn't told me?

HORACE: No Ma'am.

CORELLA: Are you sure?

HORACE: Yes Ma'am.

CORELLA: I keep thinking I'm going to die. That this is one operation I won't recover from.

HORACE: Of course you will recover.

CORELLA: I don't want to die just yet, I know that. Lily Dale needs me so, Son. I just worry about her so. I used to worry about you, but now you're married to Elizabeth and you have such a happy home and you're able at least to make a living for your wife and sweet children. I don't worry so much about you now. You're a wonderful wife to him, Elizabeth.

ELIZABETH: Oh, I don't know about that.

CORELLA: I know. And it gives me a great deal of happiness. I wish Lily Dale were content. Will is a sweet boy. I wish she could be happy in her marriage like you two are and not worry all the time about being a compóser and getting rich and famous. (*She closes her eyes.*) I am getting sleepy now. Kiss me goodbye. Both of you. Pray for me.

(*They kiss her.*)

Hold me tight, Son. I don't want to die.

HORACE (*holding her*): You're not going to die.

CORELLA: Will you both be here in the morning for the operation?

HORACE: Yes.

CORELLA: And will you come in and see me afterwards as soon as they let you?

HORACE: Yes Ma'am.

CORELLA: Your father drove you over, didn't he?

ELIZABETH: Yes, he did.

CORELLA: How is your sweet mother?

ELIZABETH: She's fine.

CORELLA: She's watching the children?

ELIZABETH: Yes, she is.

CORELLA: We were very· close. Did you ever know that when your mother first moved to Harrison to work in the courthouse she boarded right across from our house and we . . .

HORACE: She's heard that, Mama.

CORELLA: I expect she has.

(CORELLA *closes her eyes. They wait for a moment to make sure she is asleep, and then they go quietly out as the lights fade.*)

(*The lights are brought up on the waiting room.* PETE *is there alone. He is reading the paper.* HORACE *and* ELIZABETH *come in.*)

HORACE: She's asleep.

PETE: Is she? How did she seem?

HORACE: I think she wanted to sleep badly, don't you, Elizabeth?

ELIZABETH: Oh, yes. I do.

PETE: How were her spirits? Did she seem worried?

HORACE: She's worried.

PETE: She worries all the time. That's part of her trouble, I think.

(*Pause.*)

HORACE: I think she's scared.

PETE: I guess so.

HORACE: The doctors really don't know what's wrong?

PETE: No.

(*Pause.*)

HORACE: How are your people?

PETE: What people?

HORACE: Your people in Atlanta, Georgia.

PETE: They're all right.

HORACE: Been back lately?

PETE: No.

HORACE: I did a lot of traveling, you know. I was on the road as a salesman before I married Elizabeth.

PETE: Did you get to Atlanta?

HORACE: No. I never got that far.

PETE: I prefer Houston now.

HORACE: You do?

PETE: I didn't use to, but I do now.

ELIZABETH: Where's my father?

PETE: Oh, I forgot to tell you. He went on over to his sister-in-law's, he said, to spend the night. He said to call him there later.

ELIZABETH: Thank you.

PETE: Your Cousin Minnie called you again. Will told her you were with your mama and couldn't be disturbed. Lily Dale and Cousin Monty and Cousin Lola and Will went out for coffee. They'll be back later, they said. You and Elizabeth are going over to Lily and Will's to spend the night and I'll go on back to our house. Lily Dale's going to sleep here. They are going to put a cot in her mother's room for her. I'm waiting now to talk one last time with the doctor.

HORACE: Does the doctor think the operation will help?

PETE: He's making no promises; he just says he hopes it will. (*Pause.*) She's not well, you know. She doesn't like to complain to me. But I know she feels badly a great deal of the time.

(LILY DALE, WILL, MONTY, *and* LOLA *come in.*)

LILY DALE: Is Mama asleep?

HORACE: Yes.

LILY DALE: How long has she been asleep?

HORACE: Not long.

LILY DALE: I pray she sleeps through the night.

PETE: She can't do that. The doctor is coming by to see her one more time, he said. She'll have to wake up to let him examine her.

LOLA: Maybe not. Maybe he'll just look at her chart and let her sleep on. She's being awful brave, isn't she?

LILY DALE: Yes, she is.

LOLA: Bless her sweet heart.

MONTY: Horace, we've been having a discussion about Cousin Lewis. I was trying to explain to Lola how you were kin to him. Let's see if I have it straight. Your grandfather and his grandmother were brother and sister, so his mother and your mother were first cousins and that makes him your mother's what?

LOLA: That's not what I want to hear about. Lily Dale was

trying to explain to me about your grandfather being cheated out of land and jewels and silver and houses.

LILY DALE: And money, too.

LOLA: How was that?

HORACE: I swear I don't remember.

LOLA: You don't?

HORACE: No.

LILY DALE: Well, I remember. Grandpa used to talk about it all the time. He was very bitter about it. I know that. You remember how bitter he was about it all, Brother?

HORACE: Yes, I remember that. But that's all past and what can you do about it?

LOLA: It would make me furious if something like that had happened in my family. I can't stand injustice of any kind. I would do something about it, let me tell you.

HORACE: What?

LOLA: Something!

MONTY: You wouldn't do anything at all. What would you do about something that happened fifty years ago?

LOLA: I'd do something!

MONTY: What?

LOLA: I'd tell everybody in town what kind of people they are. I'd make them ashamed of themselves.

MONTY: Who?

LOLA: The ones that did it.

MONTY: They're all dead. How are you going to make them ashamed? (*Pause.*) Did you hear about Cousin Otis?

LOLA: Who is Cousin Otis?

MONTY: He's a distant cousin that lives over in Brazoria County.

LOLA: Have I ever met him?

MONTY: I don't believe so.

LOLA: What did he do?

MONTY: Who?

LOLA: Your Cousin Otis.

MONTY: What do you mean, what did he do?

LOLA: You were just asking us if we'd heard about him.

MONTY: Oh, yes. Well, he got wind of all the leasing activity in the county by the big oil companies and he came over to the courthouse before they got here with their agents. And he went around to every nigra and poor white that owned a piece of land of any kind in the east part of Harrison County, and for nothing he bought up all the mineral rights on all the land out that way. And when the big oil companies came around, they had to lease the mineral rights from him. He's made millions for himself in profits.

LOLA: That's not right. Do you think that's right?

MONTY: It may not be right, but it's legal. You don't always get rich by being right.

WILL: Cousin Minnie called you again, Horace. She said not to call her back now tonight. She's going to bed.

HORACE: I'll call her in the morning.

WILL: She said she won't be there in the morning. She is going to church early and will be in church all day, except when she is in a restaurant to eat her dinner. She said she is coming over to Harrison to see you before long, as she has some facts to put before you.

LILY DALE: I'm glad I won't be there to hear them. I don't care if I ever see Minnie again as long as I live.

LOLA (*to* MONTY): You're not kin to her, are you?

MONTY: No. Thank God!

LILY DALE: She was my father's niece.

LOLA: How long has your father been dead?

LILY DALE: Oh, I don't know. How long, Brother?

HORACE: I was twelve when he died. I'm thirty-five now.

LOLA: Twenty-three years. Mercy! Do you remember your father at all?

LILY DALE: Of course we do. At least I do. Don't you, Brother?

HORACE: Yes.

LILY DALE: Pete and Mama have been married twenty-three years.

LOLA: Is that possible? Of course, they've been married ever since I've been in the family. I barely remember your father. How long had your father and mother been married before he died?

HORACE: Twelve or thirteen years.

LILY DALE: She was just a girl when she married him.

PETE: Lily Dale, go quietly and look in on your mother. She may need us for something.

LILY DALE: All right.

LOLA: And we have to go. We'll be back tomorrow.

MONTY: Good night, you all.

WILL: Maybe we should be going, too.

HORACE: I thought I might stay here, too, tonight.

LILY DALE: There is no need for that, Brother. I'm going to be here. I'm so anxious for you to see my pretty new house.

LOLA: I'm dying to see it, too.

LILY DALE: Then why don't you drive over now with Will and Brother and Elizabeth and see it.

LOLA: Is it too late, Monty?

MONTY: I don't think so.

LOLA: We'll do it then. Good night.

MONTY: Good night.

LILY DALE: Good night.

(WILL *kisses his wife goodbye.* LILY DALE *kisses her brother and* ELIZABETH *goodbye.*)

I'll call you if I need anything.

(HORACE, ELIZABETH, *and* WILL *leave.* LILY DALE *turns to* PETE. *He has his head in his hands.*)

LILY DALE: Are you worried about all the expenses?

PETE: No. I'll sell the house if I have to. I'm worried about her. I just hope this operation makes her feel better.

LILY DALE: Well, she can't feel any worse.

PETE: That's true.

LILY DALE: My last operation certainly helped me.

PETE: That's true.

LILY DALE: Did Daddy and I tell you we went to a fortune-teller who told me I was going to be a great success and make lots of money composing music and be very famous?

PETE: No.

LILY DALE: Well, she did.

PETE: I hope it's true.

LILY DALE: I know it's true. I just feel it.

(HORACE *comes in.*)

Did you forget something, Brother?

HORACE: No. I just want to stay here tonight.

LILY DALE: You can't sleep in Mama's room, Brother. You saw how small it is. They can only get a cot for me in there.

HORACE: I know. I'll just sleep out here.

PETE: Are you afraid she's not going to live during the night? Has the doctor told you anything he hasn't told us?

HORACE: No. No. I'll just feel better being here, is all. I'll sleep out here.

LILY DALE: I'm so disappointed you won't get to see my house. I wanted you so to see it.

HORACE: I'll see it tomorrow before I leave.

PETE: Are you going back tomorrow?

HORACE: Yes, if Mama is all right.

LILY DALE: Did you hear about the fortuneteller I went to, Brother?

HORACE: No.

LILY DALE: She told me I was going to be a rich and famous composer of music. She said my popular compositions were going to make me rich and my classical compositions were going to bring me fame. You and Elizabeth should go and see her, Brother, while you're in Houston. Cousin Lola and Cousin Monty can't wait to get to her. I bet she could give you wonderful business advice. She told Will he was going to make all kinds of money. She said he had money written all over his palms. I have her name and address if you want it.

HORACE: I don't believe in that kind of foolishness.

LILY DALE: Well, I don't think it's foolishness. She told me in nine months I'm going to have my whole life changed. Drastically, she said. "Oh, I hope," I said, "I'm not going to have another baby." "No," she said, "this is an artistic change. The whole world is going to hear of you," she said. "In nine months?" I said. "That will be the beginning," she said, "of great, great things." (*Pause.*) Brother, why doesn't Elizabeth like me?

HORACE: She likes you.

LILY DALE: I don't think so. It's been a great disappointment to me, let me tell you. I've never had a sister, you know. I was so hoping we could be close as sisters. I've gone out of my way to be nice to her.

NURSE (*coming in*): Mrs. Kidder?

LILY DALE: Yes.

NURSE: Your mother wants you.

LILY DALE: Oh, I thought she was asleep.

NURSE: She was, but she woke up when the doctor stopped in to see her.

LILY DALE: Where is he?

NURSE: He's gone.

LILY DALE: Did he say everything was all right?

NURSE: Yes. The operation is still scheduled for in the morning. But he wants her quiet, so if you're going to sleep in her room you'd better come along. We have your cot in place.

LILY DALE: All right.

(*She follows the* NURSE *out. There is silence in the room after they leave.*)

HORACE: Are you staying the night, too?

PETE: I don't know what to do. (*Pause.*) I guess I will stay. It will be awful lonely at the house.

(*They both are seated now. They close their eyes to sleep as the lights fade.*)

(The lights are brought up on the waiting room. It is the next day. ELIZABETH *is there with* LILY DALE, HORACE, WILL, *and* PETE. MONTY *and* LOLA *come in.)*

LOLA: Well, we're delighted to hear the good news.

LILY DALE: We're all so relieved. She stood the operation wonderfully, the doctor said. He thinks she will be like a new person now.

LOLA: I wasn't worried at all. I knew she was going to be all right. I had Monty up at the crack of dawn and we went out to the fortuneteller's house you told me about and I said: "Before you tell me a single thing about myself, I want to hear about Cousin Corella. How is she going to stand the operation?" "She'll be just fine," she said. "She'll have no trouble at all." "Well," I said, "that's wonderful news and while you're reading Monty's palm I'm going to phone my cousin and tell her." I did try to get you here at the hospital, but they couldn't find you. Did they give you my message?

LILY DALE: Yes, they did, and I did appreciate it so. What did she tell you about yourself?

LOLA: Oh, things you wouldn't believe. She told me we never had any children, and that I was born away from Houston, and she told Monty he had recently come into a great deal of money and she told me the name of the hospital your mama was in.

LILY DALE: She didn't!

LOLA: She did too. Didn't she, Monty?

MONTY: Yes, she did. I heard it with my own ears.

LILY DALE: Isn't that uncanny?

LOLA: And I told her I had a mother that was turning out to be a real problem because she wanted all my attention. And she said that would all soon be resolved by a trip over the water. And guess what Monty did? After he heard that he called up his Cousin Mae.

MONTY: Whose Cousin Mae?

LOLA: Yours. Horace said she was your cousin. Didn't you hear him?

MONTY: He said she was his cousin.

LOLA: Well, if she's his cousin, it stands to make sense she's your cousin, too.

MONTY: She's not mine. Go on all you want.

LOLA: Well, it really doesn't matter, does it?

MONTY: You're the one that brought it up.

LOLA: Well, I'm sorry I did. So let's, for heaven's sakes, change the subject.

MONTY: I'll be glad to.

LOLA: Now, where were we?

LILY DALE: You were saying Monty called Mae.

LOLA: Oh, yes. When he heard that fortuneteller say that about water and a trip, he said, "She read my mind. I woke up this morning thinking about a trip to Europe and wondering how you go about it. I was going to call my Cousin Mae."

MONTY: I didn't say my Cousin Mae, or any such thing. I said plain Mae like I have all my life. Mae ... M-A-E! Because she's not my cousin.

LOLA: Well, what difference does it make?

MONTY: It makes a hell of a lot of difference to me. I'm kin to enough peculiar people now without your spreading all over creation Mae is my cousin.

LOLA: I bet you're gonna find out one of these days that she is.

MONTY: I bet if I do I'm going to blow my brains out.

LOLA: Oh, Monty. He's awful. Isn't he awful? He doesn't mean that. He likes Mae. Don't you?

MONTY: I like her all right. I just wouldn't want her for my cousin is all, if I can help it.

LOLA: Anyway, he said the fortuneteller was a regular mind reader because he had been intending to call Mae and ask her how you went about taking a trip to Europe.

MONTY: She goes to Europe you know, like we go to Houston. She's been something like eight times, she said.

LOLA: She has mother problems, too, you know. She said her mother was driving her crazy. She said the only place her mother couldn't get at her was in Europe. She said her mother was scared of water, so she'll never cross the ocean. I said, "My mama isn't scared of anything and if she can get the money together she'll follow me to Europe or anyplace."

MONTY: Well, you don't have to worry. She'll never get the money together. Lola has a brother that takes every nickel her mother has for drink. He is drunk day and night.

LOLA: Now, don't be discussing my family's secrets. Mercy!

LILY DALE: Don't be ashamed, Lola. We all have relatives that drink. Every one of us. My father did, you know. That's why Mama had to leave him. And I guess you know, Brother, Mama and I used to worry to death when we heard tales of your drinking.

MONTY: Horace doesn't drink now. Cousin Horace is one of the hardest-working fellows I know.

LOLA: Monty is always saying that about you, Cousin Horace. He admires you a great deal. He was disappointed when you didn't invest in the oil pool with him.

MONTY: I would have made him a rich man.

LOLA: Money isn't everything now, Monty.

MONTY: That's very true.

LILY DALE: I can tell you this, though, when we heard Brother was drinking, we were worried to death . . . with his background and all. (*Pause.*) Will has a brother that drinks, you know. He's almost driven his mother crazy.

LOLA: Worried you, too, Cousin Will, I know.

WILL: Shoot, don't worry me. Nothing worries me. I said to Carlos . . .

LILY DALE (*interrupting*): That's Will's brother's name . . . Vernon Carlos. They call him Carlos. A lot of people just call him Carl. Will has no patience at all with him.

WILL: I sure don't. I said to him: "If you want to drink and kill yourself, go right ahead, but don't expect me to lose any sleep over it." I don't lose sleep over damn fools.

LILY DALE: Will has no patience with Mother Kidder either.

LOLA: Is that what you call Will's mother? Mother Kidder?

LILY DALE: Yes.

LOLA: Isn't that sweet? Does she look like you, Will?

WILL: I don't know.

LILY DALE: No. None of them look like Will. He's the handsomest one in the family.

WILL: Shoot, she just wants to get another baby grand piano out of me.

LILY DALE: What would I do with another baby grand piano? I already have the finest in Houston.

WILL: She does, too.

LOLA: I know it. Oh, we just loved your house, honey.

LILY DALE: Thank you. How did you like it, Elizabeth?

ELIZABETH: It's beautiful.

LILY DALE: Now promise me, Brother, you'll stop by on your way home.

HORACE: I promise.

PETE (*looking at his watch*): Your mother should be coming out of the ether about now. Maybe we should go look in on her, Lily Dale.

LILY DALE: All right.

(*They start out.*)

HORACE: Maybe I'll come along, too, Sister, because we're going to have to leave for home in a little.

LILY DALE: All right. I'll go into the room first and see how she is. Then you all can come in.

(*She starts out. They follow after her as the lights fade. The lights are brought up on Corella's room. She has her eyes closed. A* NURSE *sits near her.* LILY DALE *comes into the room.*)

LILY DALE (*whispering*): How is she?

NURSE: She is coming along. She's conscious now. She was asking for you.

(LILY DALE *goes over to the bed. The* NURSE *leaves.*)

LILY DALE: Mama.

CORELLA (*opening her eyes*): Mary . . .

LILY DALE: No, this isn't Mary, Mama. Aunt Mary is dead.

CORELLA: Minnie?

LILY DALE: No, my God, Mama! I'm not Minnie!

(HORACE *and* PETE *come in.* LILY DALE *whispers.*) She's still under the influence of that ether. She thought I was her sister Mary, at first, and then she thought I was Cousin Minnie.

(CORELLA *opens her eyes. She sees* PETE.)

CORELLA: Papa. You know Horace Robedaux. He's invited me to a picnic down at the river. (*She looks up at* HORACE.) I just can't bear it, Horace. I can't bear to have the children see you this way. I'm taking them home to Papa. He said I could come home and bring my children home. He said I would always have a roof over my head as long as he lived. Cousin Val, how long has Mary been dead? I was dreaming of Mary all during the operation. I was dreaming of Mary and Papa.

(*She looks up at* PETE.)

I dreamt you were dead, Papa. I dreamed you were dead and Mary was dead and Mama.

(*The* NURSE *comes in.*)

LILY DALE: I think she's out of her head.

NURSE: Oh, she'll be all right. She's just confused. They're always this way when the ether is wearing off.

CORELLA: Lily Dale . . .

LILY DALE (*going toward* CORELLA): Yes Mama?

CORELLA: Where is Horace?

LILY DALE: Right here, Mama.

CORELLA: Right where?

LILY DALE: Right beside me.

CORELLA: Who is the other man?

LILY DALE: That's your sweet husband, Mother.

CORELLA: Is that Pete?

LILY DALE: Yes.

CORELLA: Hello, Pete.

PETE: Hello.

CORELLA: I hope those operations don't break us, Pete.

PETE: We'll manage.

CORELLA: Horace . . .

HORACE: Yes Ma'am.

CORELLA: How are you making it, Son? Having to take care of a wife and two children.

HORACE: I'm managing.

CORELLA: I hope you and Elizabeth have no more children. Two is enough responsibility. (*Pause.*) You lost a child, didn't you, Son?

HORACE: Yes.

CORELLA: A little girl?

HORACE: Yes.

CORELLA: Her name was Jenny, wasn't it?

HORACE: Yes.

CORELLA: I never got to see her. She died before we could get down to visit. We felt so bad about that. Didn't we, Lily Dale?

LILY DALE: Yes Ma'am. We all had the flu you know, too.

PETE: I didn't get it. I was the only one in the family that didn't. All my relatives in Atlanta had it, too.

HORACE: Brother Vaughn didn't get it either.

CORELLA: Who?

HORACE: Brother Vaughn. Elizabeth's brother.

CORELLA: Where is he now, Son?

HORACE: In Germany.

CORELLA: Mercy! What's he doing way over there?

HORACE: He went over on a cotton boat.

CORELLA: Does he still drink?

HORACE: Yes'm. I think so.

CORELLA: Do you still drink, Son?

HORACE: Mama, you know I don't.

CORELLA: Don't ever start it again. Your father was struck down by it. Pete doesn't drink, you know. He doesn't smoke either. When he asked me to marry him, I said: "I have one question to ask you. Do you drink?" "No," he said, "I never did. Don't smoke either. I never had time for either," he said. "I been too busy making a living." "Well then, I'll marry you," I said. (*Pause.*) Pete is a fine man, Son. He's been so good to me.

NURSE (*coming to* CORELLA): Now, that's enough now. You all will have to go.

CORELLA: My daughter, too? Can't she stay?

NURSE: Well, all right. If you promise not to talk to each other.

CORELLA: We promise, don't we, Lily Dale?

LILY DALE: Yes we do.

HORACE (*coming over to the bed*): I'll be saying goodbye now, Mama.

CORELLA: Are you going back to Harrison?

HORACE: In a little.

CORELLA: Take care of yourself.

HORACE: Yes Ma'am. You take care of yourself.

(*He and* PETE *start away.*)

CORELLA: Who is that, honey?

LILY DALE: Who, Mama?

CORELLA: That man that spoke to me just now. He looks so much like my papa.

LILY DALE: That's Horace, Mama.

CORELLA: My husband?

LILY DALE: No Ma'am, your son.

CORELLA: My son is that old?

LILY DALE: Yes Ma'am.

CORELLA (*reaching her hand out weakly*): Son . . .

(*He comes back to the bed.*)

Where do you live now?

HORACE: Harrison.

CORELLA: That's right. So you do. And you have two children and a wife?

HORACE: Yes Ma'am.

CORELLA: That's good and now I have it all straight.

(*The* NURSE *motions to* HORACE *and* PETE *to leave. They do so.* CORELLA *closes her eyes.* LILY DALE *sits beside her as the lights fade.*)

(*The lights are brought up on* GORDON *in the store. It is two months later, mid-December, and it is raining. A black man,* SYLVESTER MALONE *comes into the store.*)

GORDON: Good morning, Sylvester.

SYLVESTER: Good morning. Raining again.

GORDON: Let it rain. Now the cotton crop is ruined, let it rain.

SYLVESTER: I get tired of the rain.

GORDON: You live in the wrong part of the country then.

SYLVESTER: I know. The Gulf Coast is a rainy place. Shoot, forty days and forty nights . . . more like ninety days and ninety nights. Noah had nothing on us. Keeps on, we're going to have to all buy arks. Mr. Horace not here?

GORDON: No. He went to the bank on a little business.

SYLVESTER: Well, I stopped by to see him on a little business, too. I was supposed to pay out my suit this month, but I can't cut it. It's going to have to be early January now, it looks like. But tell him not to sell my suit on me, please. I will be by in here for sure in early January and pay out the balance.

GORDON: I will tell him.

(SYLVESTER *goes. His eyes closed,* GORDON *leans against the table stacked with clothes. He begins to doze, his head falls forward, waking him up. He changes his position, then repeats the whole process over again. And this time as he wakes up,* HORACE *comes in. He has an umbrella, which he lowers as he comes in.*)

GORDON: A good day for ducks. I hope we don't have a flood.

HORACE: I don't think there is any danger of that yet.

GORDON: I wish I had been here the time the Brazos, the Benard, and the Colorado all flooded at the same time. They say there were five counties like a solid lake of water.

HORACE: That's what they say.

GORDON: Mr. Vaughn is doing a lot of work on getting the raft out of the river, I know. They say once that is done the flood danger will be behind us. Isn't Brother Vaughn due back today?

HORACE: Yes. He gets in on the afternoon train.

GORDON: Everybody is coming home . . . Cousin Monty and Cousin Lola got in from Europe last night, Mama said. We got a card from them from Paris this morning and they were already home. What time are Cousin Will and Cousin Lily Dale bringing your mama?

HORACE: They should have been here an hour ago.

GORDON: I expect the bad roads slowed them up. I hope that new Packard of Cousin Will's didn't get stuck on its way here. Have you had a ride in his Packard yet?

HORACE: Yes.

GORDON: When did you ride in it?

HORACE: When I was at the hospital when Mama was being operated on.

GORDON: Oh, yes. It's wonderful she's had such a quick recovery, isn't it?

HORACE: Yes it is.

GORDON: Mama went down on the train to see her last week and she says she looks just fine. She saw Cousin Lily Dale's new house, too. She said it was a regular palace. Have you seen it?

HORACE: Yes, I saw it when I was visiting Mama.

GORDON: Mama says Cousin Lily Dale was excited because some big music publisher was talking about publishing all her music. She says Uncle Will had to agree to put two thousand dollars up, but the publisher thinks they will just sell like hotcakes once he can get them to the public. And he guarantees to make Cousin Lily Dale all kinds of money. (*Pause.*) Sylvester Malone was in here just now. He said he would have to wait until next month to get his suit out. He looks awful ragged, poor thing. I felt sorry for him.

HORACE: There's no work at all in the county because of the rain. Anybody else in while I was gone?

GORDON: Oh, yes. I almost forgot. Cousin Lester Higgins came in. He said he wanted to see the hat case Cousin Lewis kicked in that time. And I showed it to him. And he said Cousin Lewis was in Galveston taking the Keeley Cure and did I know how much it cost to have the glass case fixed? I said I didn't but you were at the bank on business, and he said: "What's he doing, borrowing money?" real sarcastic-like. And I said I didn't know what you were doing as you didn't tell me your business and I didn't ever ask. And then he said while he was waiting he had some shopping to do in town and would I cash a check for him for a hundred dollars, to save him a trip to the bank. But I was too quick for him and I remembered you said the last time you cashed a check for him it bounced and you like to never get your money back. So I said, "I'm sorry, Cousin Lester, I don't have that much in the cash register." "How much do you have?" he said. "Maybe five dollars," I said. "Well, I'll write a check out for that amount," he said. I said: "I'm sorry, sir, but I can't do it. That's cash and if someone bought something needing change, I would be in a sure enough mess." "What kind of a store does he run here?" he said. And he left mad as anything.

HORACE: Well, you did right.

GORDON: Thank you. But just as he was leaving, Cousin Lewis came in and he looked drunk to me. And Cousin Lester said, what the hell was he doing home from Galveston? And they went out, arguing like everything. I was afraid they might get into a fight and break another showcase. I was relieved when they went on down the street. I didn't want anything else bad to happen while I was in charge here.

(MONTY *and* LOLA *come in.*)

HORACE: Well, look who's here. Welcome.

MONTY: And we are glad to get home.

LOLA: Mae can have Europe. I was sick all the way over there. And all the way back.

MONTY: You talk about storms. You think you've seen storms here on the Gulf Coast? The 1900 storm was nothing to what we went through twice.

LOLA: I said: "Mae, why didn't you tell us it was the storm season?" "I thought you knew," she said. "They don't bother me." "Well, they bother me," I said. They'll never get me out on that water again for anything.

GORDON: Where did you go?

MONTY: God only knows. We went everyplace.

GORDON: I got a postcard from you this morning.

LOLA: Where was it from?

GORDON: Paris.

(*She makes a face.*) Didn't you like Paris?

LOLA: No. Mae loves it. She said: "Just wait until you see Paris. You'll never want to leave." Well, I saw it and I couldn't wait to get away.

MONTY: England was the only place I liked because I knew what they were talking about.

LOLA: Well, you may have, but I didn't. I couldn't understand half of what they said in English.

MONTY: We didn't get to see the king and queen.

LOLA: We were so disappointed about that. Mae told another lie about that, too. She said you saw them every place you went over there. And we didn't see them once.

MONTY: And we paid a man fifteen dollars to take us to where they were going to appear. But he never showed up. Took our fifteen dollars and we never saw that four-flusher again.

LOLA: That's all they are in Europe, four-flushers. I said to Monty, "That's why Mae likes it over there so much. She's married five four-flushers herself." She must like them, marrying so many. I bet she's over there right now looking for another four-flusher to marry.

(WILL, CORELLA, LILY DALE, *and* PETE *come into the area.*)

WILL: Well, look who is here.

MONTY: And glad to be here, let me tell you.

LOLA: Don't anybody ever talk you into getting on that ocean. I don't care how big the boat is.

(LOLA *kisses* CORELLA *and* LILY DALE.)

I'm so glad to see you both. Why Cousin Corella, you look well. Like you never had a sick day in your life. How do you feel?

CORELLA: Just fine.

WILL: She's getting fat.

CORELLA: I sure hope not.

LOLA: And Lily Dale, Cousin Inez was telling me all about you having your music published. We were just thrilled. I'm going to buy me a copy of every one of your songs.

MONTY: I can't wait until somebody makes Victrola recordings of them so we could listen to them.

LOLA: I want them now. I don't care if I can read the notes or not. I can read the words and you wrote all the words, too, didn't you, honey?

LILY DALE: All except the classical pieces. They don't have words. Only the popular songs have words.

LOLA: My special favorite has always been "A Square Peg in a Round Hole." They published that one, too, I hope?

CORELLA: Well, Lola. We've had a little disappointment about all that.

LOLA: You have?

CORELLA: Lily Dale's publisher turned out not to be a music publisher at all.

LOLA: What was he?

WILL: Just a fast-talking crook. He took my two thousand dollars and that was the last we've heard of him.

MONTY: Same thing happened to me in London. I gave a man—a nice, refined-looking man, wasn't he, Lola?

LOLA: You thought so.

MONTY: You thought so, too, at the time.

LOLA: I did not. I never trusted him for a single moment.

MONTY: Well, I did trust him. I gave him fifteen dollars of good American money.

LOLA: It was English money.

MONTY (*snarling*): I know that, but it was fifteen dollars' worth of American money. God knows how much it was of English money. I never could keep straight how they count their money.

LOLA: They don't say dollars, you know. They say pounds and you better not give them a dollar because they'll give it right back to you. And they are always cheating you because they can think faster in their money than you can. By the time you've figured up what you are paying for a thing in dollars and cents they have taken your money and gone.

MONTY: Anyway, I gave this man I trusted fifteen dollars to take us where we could see the king and queen. The morning he was to take us he never showed up.

GORDON: Who didn't show up?

MONTY: The man didn't. The man I gave the fifteen dollars to.

GORDON: Did the king show up?

MONTY: How the hell do I know if the king showed up or not? I weren't there to see.

GORDON: Where were you?

MONTY: At my hotel waiting for the damn man I gave the fifteen dollars to. It takes away all your faith in human nature.

(LILY DALE *cries and goes out of the store.*)

CORELLA: Oh, Will. Go after her. Don't let her cry.

(*He goes.*)

Poor thing. Her heart is just broken with disappointment. The Arts Club was giving a recital of her songs in her honor and to announce their publication date, and Mr. Regan was to be there with her and to tell them all the exciting details.

LOLA: Who is Mr. Regan, honey?

CORELLA: He was the publisher. Well, he was supposed to have been one. One o'clock came and he didn't show up. And one-thirty came and no Mr. Regan; two o'clock and no Mr. Regan. So they decided to go ahead and sing and play her songs. And he never came at all. Will immediately began to check on him and everything he told us was a lie, a plain lie. He had checked out of the Milby Hotel the day before and they didn't know where he came from or where he had gone to. Will tried to stop payment on his check, but it was too late.

(ELIZABETH *comes in.*)

Hello, honey.

(*They kiss.*)

ELIZABETH: Hello, Monty. Hello, Lola. Welcome home.

MONTY: Thank you.

LOLA: We're glad to get here, let me tell you. We didn't like Europe at all.

ELIZABETH: You didn't?

LOLA: Not one single bit. Did we, Monty?

MONTY: No. Give me the good old U.S.A. anytime.

LOLA: All their food is so rich.

MONTY: And so expensive.

LOLA: I hear Brother Vaughn is coming in today.

ELIZABETH: He was supposed to. He was due in on the afternoon train from Galveston, but he missed it.

LOLA: How did he like Europe?

ELIZABETH: He only saw Germany. He loved it.

LOLA: He can have it.

WILL (*coming in*): Lily Dale is going to wait in the car. She has one of her headaches.

CORELLA: Those headaches of hers worry me to death. She has them too often.

LOLA: Did you hear about her disappointment, Elizabeth?

ELIZABETH: No.

LOLA: Her music publisher turned out to be a crook.

ELIZABETH: Oh, I'm sorry.

WILL: I lost two thousand dollars in the deal.

MONTY: Well, Will, next time you'll know better.

WILL: Lily Dale is about to drive me crazy. She wants me to drop all my work at the wholesale house and take her and her music into New York to see about getting it published.

LOLA: Well, that's where they do publish the music, Will.

MONTY: Maybe you could send it to them and save yourself the trip.

WILL: We've already sent it to ten different places. They all sent it back.

LOLA: Did you send "A Square Peg in a Round Hole"? Or is it "A Round Peg in a Square Hole"?

CORELLA: It's "A Square Peg in a Round Hole."

WILL: Yes, we did. We sent that one, too. They sent it back along with the others.

CORELLA: Sister doesn't think they even look at them.

MONTY: She may be right.

LOLA: I tell you, I think if Gene Austin ever made a recording of "A Square Peg in a Round Hole," it would sweep the country.

CORELLA: Tell that to Lily Dale. It might encourage her.

LOLA: I will.

GORDON: You all are having dinner at my house, I believe. Mama fried four chickens. Brother said: "No wonder we are almost in the poorhouse, Mother. You feed all the relatives when they come to town." He was joking, of course.

LOLA: Of course he was. I can just see Cousin Leonard saying that.

GORDON: Cousin Horace, if you and Cousin Elizabeth can go over, Mama says you're welcome too.

HORACE: No, Son, it's Saturday. I don't like to leave the store on a Saturday.

ELIZABETH: I'll just stay here and have a hamburger with Horace.

GORDON: Do you mind if I go then?

HORACE: No. Go right ahead.

(CORELLA *kisses* HORACE.)

CORELLA: We'll see you later, Son.

HORACE: Yes Ma'am.

(CORELLA *kisses* ELIZABETH. *She leaves with* WILL, LOLA, MONTY, *and* GORDON.)

ELIZABETH: Any business?

HORACE: No. I think I've taken in eighty cents all morning.

ELIZABETH: Try not to get discouraged.

HORACE: I'm not. What can I do about it? It's all out of my hands. We just didn't make a crop again this year is all. (*Pause.*) This rain is about to drive me crazy.

ELIZABETH: I know. I wish it would quit now. (*Pause.*) We're going to make it.

HORACE: I'm not worried. I know we are. (*Pause.*) I went over to the bank and they loaned me some money. For another six months. They were real nice about it. They said they knew I was trying as hard as I could and that none of this was my fault.

ELIZABETH: It certainly isn't. (*Pause.*) Papa's in a state. Mama has had an asthma attack. Aunt Lizzie called from Houston. The reason Brother missed the train for Galveston was he got drunk as soon as he got off the boat and went into Houston and began calling all the relatives and just talking like a crazy man, Papa said. Anyway, I got a nurse to take care of the children and I cleared out.

HORACE: You spend the afternoon here with me.

ELIZABETH: I'm going to.

HORACE: How are the children?

ELIZABETH: They are wonderful.

HORACE: Are you hungry?

ELIZABETH: Yes.

HORACE: You watch the store while I go and get us hamburgers.

ELIZABETH: All right.

(*He starts out.*)

Horace.

(*He turns.*)

I love you.

HORACE: I love you.

(*He takes her in his arms. He kisses her. He holds her for a moment.*)

ELIZABETH: Today is Jenny's birthday.

HORACE: I know.

ELIZABETH: I thought later I'd walk out to the cemetery and take a flowering plant of some kind. Maybe a poinsettia. (*Pause.*) I don't forget her. I remember Mrs. Huston telling me at the time I would, but I don't. It's like Mama says, you think of her differently than the others, but you think of her.

(HORACE *goes.*)

(ELIZABETH *walks to the back of the store.* MINNIE CURTIS *comes in. She has an umbrella, which she folds up.* ELIZABETH *hears her enter the store and turns and walks back.*)

ELIZABETH: May I help you?

(*Pause; then she recognizes* MINNIE.)

Miss Minnie Curtis?

MINNIE: Yes.

ELIZABETH: Horace went out for some hamburgers for us. He'll be right back. Isn't this weather terrible?

MINNIE: Yes, it is.

ELIZABETH: Was it raining in Houston?

MINNIE: Yes. Not like here. I think it rains no place like it does here. I've been here for a while. I saw that crowd of Thorntons in the store and I sure didn't want to see any of them. Bunch of frivolous fools. I'm very fond of Horace, Elizabeth.

ELIZABETH: I know you are, and we appreciate so much all you did for him while he was in business school.

MINNIE: His mother and I had a big fight in Foley's ladies' room just before she was sick. I thought maybe for a while I was the one sent her to the hospital.

ELIZABETH: I'm sure not.

MINNIE: I hope not. Anyway, I was going to tell it all to Horace. I've been trying every way in the world I could to get down here to tell him about it. I teach school, you know. I only have the weekends. So, I said this weekend I'm bound I'm going and I did, but now I got here I don't know why I came. I don't want to bother him anymore now with what happened twenty-five years ago or more. So, I almost turned around and went back, but I thought, no. He's my cousin, the cousin I'm most fond of, and I'll just go and visit with him before I go back to Houston.

ELIZABETH: I'm glad you did.

MINNIE: I know Horace has lots of cousins he's fond of, on both sides, but I don't have so many I'm fond of. There's Horace and a cousin in Arkansas I like and that's about all. Everybody in the family has always said I have a peculiar disposition, sensitive, I get my feelings hurt without reason, and I suppose that's true.

(HORACE *comes in with hamburgers and coffee.*)

Hello, Cousin.

HORACE: Well, look who's here. Cousin Minnie. You're just the one I wanted to see. I was awake half the night trying to remember Cousin Cal's oldest daughter's name.

MINNIE: Delia.

HORACE: Delia.

MINNIE: Delia lives in California.

HORACE: Does she?

MINNIE: Married and has three children. Cousin Cal is dead.

HORACE: And Cousin Mat?

MINNIE: Dead. So many are dead. So many of the cousins. Of course, there are new cousins, their children, and their children's children, but I've lost track of most of them. A family is a remarkable thing, isn't it? You belong. And then you don't. It passes you by. Unless you start a family of your own. (*Turns her head away. She is crying.*) I'm sorry. I don't know what got into me. I think it's coming back here after all these years. Why, I left here when I was seventeen and I haven't been back since. And I'm alone. I've no mother or father or sisters or brothers, no husband, no children, only cousins who don't want to fool with me. Cousins. Cousins. When I was a girl . . . (*Pause.*) Who lives in our house now?

HORACE: I swear I don't know, Cousin Minnie. I live in the opposite part of town now and I never get over towards the river anymore. I think the Geisings or some of their children still live there though, don't they, Elizabeth?

ELIZABETH: Yes, I think so.

MINNIE: When I was a girl I used to really envy the Thorntons. I could hear the music and the dancing coming from their old house up the block. What happened to the Thornton house?

HORACE: They tore it down and built a cottage for Aunt Inez when she married, and two rent houses.

MINNIE: Did they? I'd hear the music and the dancing coming from there and I would envy them so, their good times. I pretended I thought they were foolish and frivolous, and I'm sure they were, but that's really how I wanted to be, to have beaux and go to dances and play the piano and sing songs with my family. Not study Latin and Greek and worry about becoming a schoolteacher. I pretended to despise them, but I envied them. And I envied you because you were son and nephew and cousin to them. I wanted them so for my relatives.

GORDON (*coming in with a plate of food*): Mama insisted I bring some chicken at least to you all. (*He sees* MINNIE.) Oh, excuse me.

HORACE: Gordon, this is my Cousin Minnie. She used to live here. She lives in Houston now.

GORDON: How do you do? Are we cousins, too?

HORACE: No. She's kin to me on the Robedaux side.

MINNIE: My mother and his father were brother and sister. We're first cousins, Horace and I.

GORDON: We're first cousins, too. My mother and his mother were sisters.

MINNIE: I know. I know them all well.

GORDON: I'll tell her I saw you. I know my mama would want to be remembered to you.

MINNIE: Thank you.

GORDON: Would you like to come out to the house and see everybody?

MINNIE: No, thank you. I have to leave in a few minutes. I have to take the two o'clock train to Houston.

GORDON: Let me drive you. I have my car out here. You shouldn't walk in this rain.

MINNIE: I don't want to put you out.

GORDON: You won't be.

MINNIE: Well, thank you.

HORACE: You sure you have to go?

MINNIE: Yes. I have to be home before dark. I have things to do.

(LEWIS *enters. He is drunk.* GORDON *goes up to him.*)

GORDON: Yes, Cousin Lewis. What can I do for you?

LEWIS: I'm looking for a cousin of mine.

GORDON: Which one, Cousin Lewis?

LEWIS: Jamie Dale.

GORDON: Cousin Lewis, you're a little mixed up. Jamie Dale isn't with us anymore. He's dead.

(GORDON *turns to* HORACE *and* ELIZABETH, *whispering.*)

Mama just told us when we went to the house that late yesterday afternoon Jamie's mama, Miss Velma, took a tombstone over to the cemetery and put it on Jamie's grave. She had written on it: "Jamie Dale, murdered by his cousin, Lewis Higgins." She said some of our prominent citizens called on Miss Velma this morning and pleaded with her until she agreed to have "murdered by his cousin, Lewis Higgins" taken off the tombstone.

LEWIS: My name is Lewis Higgins. What the hell are you talking about Lewis Higgins?

MINNIE: I'm going to have to leave or I'm going to miss my train.

GORDON: Yes Ma'am.

(MINNIE *takes Elizabeth's hand.*)

MINNIE: Goodbye, Elizabeth.

ELIZABETH: Goodbye, Miss Minnie.

HORACE: Goodbye, Cousin Minnie.

MINNIE: Call me sometime when you're in Houston.

(*She and* GORDON *leave.*)

LEWIS: Who's that?

HORACE: My cousin. Minnie Curtis.

LEWIS: Is she my cousin?

HORACE: No.

LEWIS: Who are you?

HORACE: Horace.

LEWIS: Are you my cousin?

HORACE: Yes.

LEWIS: Doggone. (*Pause.*) I never cussed in front of a lady in my life unless I was so drunk I didn't know it. Were you all kin to Jamie Dale?

HORACE: No.

LEWIS: He was my cousin. I killed him. I feel so bad about it, but it was him or me. I killed my cousin, my cousin Jamie Dale. He didn't care how he talked in front of ladies, you know. (*To* HORACE:) And you're my cousin?

HORACE: Yes.

LEWIS (*to* ELIZABETH): Who are you?

ELIZABETH: Elizabeth.

LEWIS: Are we kin?

ELIZABETH: No.

LEWIS: Does Brother Vaughn still work here?

HORACE: No.

LEWIS: Where is he?

HORACE: In Houston.

LEWIS: What's he doing there?

HORACE: On his way home.

LEWIS: Where's he been?

HORACE: Germany.

LEWIS: Is that so? What did he go to Germany for?

HORACE: He wanted to.

LEWIS: I've been to Galveston a number of times. I take the

Keeley Cure. It don't help me any. Did you ever have the Keeley Cure?

HORACE: No.

LEWIS: You're Horace, ain't you?

HORACE: Yes.

LEWIS: You used to drink, didn't you?

HORACE: Yes.

LEWIS: Did you take the Keeley Cure?

HORACE: No.

LEWIS: How did you quit?

HORACE: I just quit.

LEWIS: I've had the Keeley Cure three times. What do you have here?

HORACE: Chicken.

LEWIS: Fried chicken?

HORACE: Yes.

LEWIS: And what's that?

HORACE: Hamburgers.

LEWIS: Can I have a piece of your fried chicken?

HORACE: Help yourself.

LEWIS: I don't care for hamburgers. I love fried chicken. (*He takes a piece.*) We're cousins?

HORACE: Yes.

LEWIS: First or second?

HORACE: Second. Once removed.

LEWIS: Is that so? (*He takes a bite of his chicken.*) My chicken is good. You all have some.

(ELIZABETH *and* HORACE *take pieces of chicken. They take a bite.*)

(*To* ELIZABETH:) Did you cook this?

ELIZABETH: No.

LEWIS: Who did?

HORACE: My aunt.

LEWIS: Which one?

HORACE: Inez.

LEWIS: Is she kin to me?

HORACE: Yes.

LEWIS: A cousin?

HORACE: Yes.

LEWIS: She cooks good chicken, doesn't she?

HORACE: Yes.

LEWIS: I have a lot of cousins. Do you?

HORACE: Yes.

LEWIS: Jamie Dale was my cousin.

HORACE: Yes.

LEWIS: He's dead. We were out with these two ladies, you know, and I hate to say it, but we were all drunk. The ladies, too, and he cursed them. I told him not to and he drew a knife. It was him or me. Cousins . . . a lot of them dead, you know. The graveyard is full of our cousins. The town is full of them. We'll be in that graveyard someday, I'll be there and you'll be there. Why, the graveyard will be full of cousins. (*There is silence.*) You're married?

ELIZABETH: Yes.

LEWIS: To each other?

ELIZABETH: Yes.

LEWIS: Congratulations. (*Starts out; at the edge of the area he turns around.*) Nice to have seen you, Cousin. Which cousin are you?

HORACE: Horace.

LEWIS: Horace.

(*He continues on his way.* ELIZABETH *and* HORACE *watch him go as the light fades.*)

The Death of Papa

Characters

HORACE ROBEDAUX, JR.

IDA HARRIS

ELIZA

GERTRUDE

ELIZABETH ROBEDAUX

MARY VAUGHN

BROTHER VAUGHN

INEZ KIRBY

CORELLA DAVENPORT

HORACE ROBEDAUX, SR.

WILL BORDEN

WALTER

Act One

Place: Harrison, Texas
Time: 1928

The lights are brought up down left revealing a section of a room in the Robedaux house. HORACE ROBEDAUX, JR., *aged ten, enters. He senses a strange kind of quiet and goes running out to the yard area down right. He stands there for a moment, listening, puzzled by the quality of the silence around him, and then goes back into the area down left.*

HORACE, JR. *(calling):* Mother . . . Mother . . . Mother . . .

(There is no answer and he stands for a beat again, listening to the silence, and then goes slowly back out into the yard. Far away a recording of a blues is heard, then it fades away and the silence again takes over as MISS IDA HARRIS *comes in.)*

IDA: Son. I've been watching for you to come home from school. Your mother is over at your grandmother's. I think she would want you over there.

HORACE, JR. *(sensing something frightening in Ida's voice):* Why?

IDA: I just think she would. So, if I were you I'd go on over there.

HORACE, JR.: Yes Ma'am.

(IDA *goes.* HORACE *doesn't leave. He sits on the ground for a moment.* IDA *reappears.*)

IDA: Horace. School has been out over an hour. Your mother will be concerned. I told her I would watch for you and tell you where to go. Now, please, go on back to your grandmother's.

(*He doesn't look at her, but runs off as the lights fade.*)

(*The lights are brought up center stage.*)

(HORACE, JR., *comes running in. Two black women,* ELIZA *and* GERTRUDE, *are there. They look glum and unhappy.* HORACE, JR. *approaches them unobtrusively. After a moment* ELIZA *sees him.*)

ELIZA: Here's Horace. Bless your heart, boy. (*To* GERTRUDE:) Run and tell Miss Elizabeth Horace is out here with me.

(GERTRUDE *disappears.*)

Isn't it terrible? I could have told them, though. I woke up this morning with this heavy heart, this heart of lead, and I thought what is the matter with you, woman? You've been saved. Your heart should be carefree. And then I looked up and I seen two mourning doves sitting on the roof of the house. Not one, but two, and I thought to myself, this is going to be a sad day for us all. "The Lord giveth and the Lord taketh away; blessed be the name of the Lord." I went for Gertrude and I told her what I'd seen. I'd no sooner finished telling her this when we heard . . .

(GERTRUDE *and* ELIZABETH ROBEDAUX *come in.* GERTRUDE *stands at the edge of the stage waiting as* ELIZABETH *runs to her son and sweeps him into her arms.*)

ELIZABETH: Son! Son! What are we going to do? What are any of us going to do?

(*She cries, holding him. He has never seen his mother cry before and it is troubling to him, and since he doesn't know the source of her grief yet, is even more disturbed.*)

GERTRUDE: He's not shedding a tear. I guess he's too young to realize what is happening.

ELIZABETH (*wiping her eyes*): His body is inside now. They just brought him home. Your grandmother is with him. She'll want to see you. Come on, honey. I have to get back in. The house is filled with people. The whole town is shocked.

(*She starts away; the boy holds back.*)

Son? . . .

(*She realizes he doesn't know yet what is going on. She goes to him again.*)

Son . . . It's your grandfather. He died of a heart attack. Quite suddenly. Dear God! Dear God! Help us all.

(*She cries again. This time the boy cries, holding her, clinging to her. After a moment they start off as* GERTRUDE *joins* ELIZA.)

ELIZA (*pointing to the roof of the house*): Yes. I come out of my house later than usual. Mr. Brother thought I was asleep, I guess, because he come out into the yard, calling: "Liza . . . Liza . . . It's time to get up. Liza . . . Liza . . ." I let him go on calling, because my heart was too heavy to answer.

Too heavy to get out of the bed. Then Mrs. Vaughn come out and she called me and I answered and was awake, and I got out of bed and dressed and opened the door and I thought this is one day I hate to see and I was halfway across the yard when I looked up and I saw the two doves flying around in the air. Stay away from here, I said to myself, stay away from us. But before I could finish those words they both descended and lit on the roof there and I knew then. Death . . . I knew would be here at this house for somebody, sometime today. And it came at one-thirty in the afternoon on the corner in front of Mr. Jack Crawford's filling station. Mr. Henry Vaughn, rich and powerful, is struck by the hand of death and lies dying on the sidewalk before any of his loved ones can get to him to say goodbye.

(*During her speech the lights are brought up on the* VAUGHN *house.* MRS. VAUGHN *is leaning over a coffin in grief.* HORACE, JR., *comes in, timidly. He watches his grandmother for a moment. He realizes she is not aware of his presence. He starts timidly toward her when* IDA *comes in and goes to* MRS. VAUGHN.)

IDA: Mary . . .

(MRS. VAUGHN *looks up and sees her friend. She says nothing.* IDA *goes to her, embracing her. Both women look down at the casket.*)

MRS. VAUGHN: Oh, my God, Ida! Oh, my God!

IDA: I'm so sorry! I'm so sorry!

(*She starts away. She sees* HORACE, JR.)

Horace . . . You understand now why I wanted you to

come over here? Have you spoken to your grandmother yet?

(HORACE *doesn't answer.*)

Go on, honey. She'll want to speak to you. But don't stay long. (*She takes his hand.*) Come on.

(*She leads* HORACE, JR., *to* MRS. VAUGHN.)

Mary . . .

(MRS. VAUGHN *doesn't look away from the coffin.*)

Here's Horace, Jr., honey . . .

(MRS. VAUGHN *looks around then and sees her grandson and reaches her arms out to him. He goes to her and* IDA *leaves.*)

MRS. VAUGHN: Oh, Horace! What are we going to do, Son?

HORACE, JR.: I'm very sorry.

MRS. VAUGHN: I know you are; he loved you, Son. He was awful proud of you.

(BROTHER VAUGHN *comes in. He stands by* HORACE *and his mother. His mother looks up at him.*)

Brother, are you drinking? My God, are you drinking at a time like this?

BROTHER: Mama . . . I just couldn't help it today. Don't you understand that?

MRS. VAUGHN: No. I don't understand it. I don't understand it at all. Who can I turn to in my sorrow if I can't turn to my son? Who is going to take his place if it's not you? It would break his heart to know you were standing over his coffin drunk.

BROTHER: Oh, God, Mama! Help me! Help me!

(BROTHER *kneels beside his mother. She is crying as* HORACE *slips away and the lights fade.*)

(*The lights are brought up on* INEZ *and* CORELLA DAVENPORT, *Horace, Jr.'s great aunt and paternal grandmother. They are dressed in dark clothes and seated on lawn chairs.*)

CORELLA (*calling*): Gertrude, when the baby wakes up from his nap bring him out to us. He should get a look at his grandfather's funeral procession even if he doesn't know what is going on.

INEZ: Where's little Horace?

CORELLA: Gertrude, where is little Horace?

GERTRUDE (*calling back*): He's in the kitchen.

INEZ: Tell him to come out on the front yard so he can see the funeral procession as it goes past.

CORELLA: They go from their house to the church; from the church to the cemetery. I guess the whole thing will take three hours.

(HORACE, JR., *appears.*)

I think everyone in town, white and black, will be in that church. They say it is the biggest funeral this town will ever see. There it starts . . . See? . . .

(*She turns to find* HORACE, JR.)

See, Horace?

(HORACE, JR., *stands by her.*)

Poor Mary was just pitiful. She said she didn't know how she could bear to say goodbye to him.

INEZ: That's not him, honey. He's not there anymore.

CORELLA: I didn't say he was. I'm only telling you how Mary feels about it.

INEZ: He was a remarkable man. He did a lot of good to a lot of people. I have my farm today because of him. After T. died I just couldn't face the debt he had left on our farm and I went to Mr. Vaughn and I said, "Mr. Vaughn, I'm going to have to turn this farm back to you." "No such thing," he said. "You'll pay it out any way you want to, any amount, as long as you want, but you are going to keep it." And I did. Thank God!

(*Pause.*)

CORELLA: There it starts. There's the hearse and there's the car with Mary and the children. I guess his brother and his children are in the second car or is it his sister?

INEZ: I think his brother and his wife and his sister are in the same car. I was so surprised when I heard about his death. I was in the backyard and I saw this Negro man running and I said, "What's the matter?" "Mr. Vaughn is dead," he said. "He just dropped over dead in front of Mr. Jack Crawford's filling station." Why, I'd never known him to have a sick day.

CORELLA: Elizabeth told me he had gone down a month before to see about some more life insurance and the doctor wouldn't pass him for it. Told him he had a serious heart condition, but he didn't say a word to anybody about it.

(*She looks about to see if* HORACE, JR., *is listening. He is, but they think he is watching the procession and not listening.*)

INEZ: I wonder how much money he left?

CORELLA: I think he left a great deal. I think there is a lot of land and there was life insurance. I understand three hundred thousand dollars in cash.

INEZ: Mercy!

CORELLA: Don't say I said that though, for God's sakes!

INEZ (*whispering*): I hope Brother will be able to take over now.

CORELLA: Poor Mary! Brother is such a disappointment.

INEZ: I know. I don't understand it. Mr. Vaughn was such a fine man. A self-made man, too. He had to work for everything he had.

(*From offstage Gertrude's voice sings "Careless Love."*)

CORELLA (*calling*): Gertrude, quiet. There's a funeral going on.

GERTRUDE (*offstage*): Yes Ma'am. I'm sorry.

CORELLA (*looking over at* HORACE, JR.): Horace, come here to your big mama.

(*He goes over to her.*)

I don't get to see him as much as I'd like to, living so far away in Houston. It's a shame we only get to see each other at sad times like this.

(HORACE, JR., *starts away.*)

Where are you going?

HORACE, JR.: To read. (*He continues on.*)

INEZ: You think he should read a book during his grand-father's funeral?

CORELLA: I don't know what to say. I wish he wasn't reading books at any time. It worries me to death. I'm afraid he is going to turn out to be like Terrence Robe-daux. And he won't be worth killing then for sure. He'll just spend his life reading books and letting other people take care of him.

INEZ: I wish we'd had some education, though. I wish Papa had made us finish school.

CORELLA: I don't know. There's good and bad in every-thing. At least we don't lie around the house and read Greek and Latin all the time and let other people feed us. Do you see the kinds of books that boy reads? A boy of ten.

INEZ: Didn't big Horace used to read?

CORELLA: Yes. And it worried me to death then, too. But fortunately he outgrew it.

INEZ: He loves newspapers.

CORELLA: Yes, he does. Whenever he hears I'm coming in from Houston for a visit he reminds me to bring him some newspapers. Rushed as I was to get here for the funeral and I had to go downtown and get him a *New York Times*, a *Chicago Tribune*, *Kansas City Star*, and *The Philadelphia Inquirer*.

INEZ: How did he ever hear of all those papers?

CORELLA: I don't know. Anyway, if he has to read I'm glad he reads something like that. If I ever caught a child of mine reading as much as Horace, Jr., does I'd grab the book out of his hands and throw it into the stove.

INEZ: Well, if it worries you so much why don't you speak to Horace, Sr., about it?

CORELLA: I'm going to. (*She gets up.*) Well, the cars have all passed. I'll go in and see about lunch for us. We have to eat, funeral or no.

(*She takes her chair and starts away.* INEZ *follows with her chair.* HORACE, JR., *enters with a book.* GERTRUDE *comes out.*)

GERTRUDE: It's so quiet. It's so quiet. Your grandfather is on the way to the graveyard. It's so quiet. So quiet. Little Horace, put that book down and talk to me.

HORACE, JR.: How old are you?

GERTRUDE: I'm eighteen. How old are you?

HORACE, JR.: Ten. How come you don't go to school?

GERTRUDE: I do.

HORACE, JR.: How come you're not there today?

GERTRUDE: The same reason you're not there. Because there is a funeral.

HORACE, JR.: He's not your grandfather.

GERTRUDE: No. That's true. But he is yours and Henry Vaughn's.

HORACE, JR.: I've got a sister that's dead. She was older than either me or Henry Vaughn and I never saw her.

(HORACE, SR., *comes in.*)

Is the funeral over?

HORACE, SR.: Yes.

HORACE, JR.: Where's Mother?

HORACE, SR.: She's over at your grandmother's.

HORACE, JR.: When is she coming home?

HORACE, SR.: In a little while.

(CORELLA *and* INEZ *come back in.*)

CORELLA: You're back . . . .

(*She kisses her son,* HORACE, SR.)

The children were just wonderful. The baby had a good long nap; he doesn't realize what's going on, poor little thing. How is Elizabeth?

HORACE, SR.: She's heartbroken, of course.

CORELLA: How is Mary?

HORACE, SR.: She was very composed until they got to the cemetery. Then she was pitiful.

HORACE, JR.: I've got two grandfathers in the graveyard now.

INEZ: Yes, you do.

HORACE, JR.: And you have a husband there.

INEZ: Yes, I do.

HORACE, JR.: And he died with the flu?

INEZ: Yes, he did.

HORACE, JR.: Were you sad when he died?

INEZ: Yes, I was. Goodness, little Horace, what do you think?

CORELLA: Where's Elizabeth?

HORACE, SR.: She's over at her mother's. There's a big crowd over there. Eating and visiting. I'm going over. I just wanted to see how everybody was over here. (*He starts away.*) Some of them that haven't seen the baby may be over after a while. Maybe you should give the baby a bath, Gertrude. Elizabeth wants him dressed up in that new suit she made him.

GERTRUDE: Yes Sir.

CORELLA: Inez and I can bathe him.

(*She and* INEZ *leave.*)

HORACE, SR.: You get dressed up, too, Horace, Jr., in case we have company.

HORACE, JR.: Yes Sir. Can I go with you over to Grandma's?

HORACE, SR.: Not now. There's too much company over there now and no place for children.

(*He goes.* GERTRUDE *picks up the book* HORACE, JR., *is reading.*)

GERTRUDE: *The Adventures of Huckleberry Finn.*

HORACE, JR.: Did you ever read that?

GERTRUDE: No.

HORACE, JR.: Did you ever read *The Adventures of Tom Sawyer*?

GERTRUDE: No.

HORACE, JR.: What books have you read?

GERTRUDE: I don't know. Not many.

HORACE, JR.: Don't you read books in your school?

GERTRUDE: No.

HORACE, JR.: Then how come you go to school?

GERTRUDE: To learn things.

HORACE, JR.: What?

GERTRUDE: To be a nurse or a teacher.

HORACE, JR.: What do you want to be that for?

GERTRUDE: To help my people.

HORACE, JR.: Who are your people? Your mama and daddy?

GERTRUDE: No. My people . . . my race. That's what Professor McCann says we're in school for. To help our race. Isn't that what you go to school for?

HORACE, JR.: I don't know. I never heard about it, if I did.

GERTRUDE: Professor McCann is as light as you are.

HORACE, JR.: Is he white?

GERTRUDE: No. He's just light. He has a son studying to be a doctor. He buys all his clothes at your daddy's store. I see him in there buying clothes almost every Saturday when I go uptown. My mama bought a shirt last Saturday at your daddy's store. She says he's a good friend to all the colored people around here. She says they all like him. So was your granddaddy. My mama went to his funeral this afternoon. I sure wanted to go, but she said I could do more good by coming over here and helping out. "But I don't want to spend my life nursing children, Mama, the way you have," I said. "No indeed. I want to be a nurse for the sick or a schoolteacher. I'm going to college."

HORACE, JR.: Where are you going?

GERTRUDE: Prairie View Normal.

HORACE, JR.: That's the colored college.

GERTRUDE: Yes, it is. Are you going to college?

HORACE, JR.: I don't know. My daddy never went to college. His daddy did, though. He was a lawyer. (*He whispers.*) My daddy was twelve when his daddy died. His mama and daddy were separated. He doesn't know I know that, but I heard him and Mama talking one night. He doesn't like the man my grandmama is married to now.

GERTRUDE: Why?

HORACE, JR.: Because he was mean to him when he was a boy. He said if his daddy had lived, his whole life would have been different. Do you think so?

GERTRUDE: I wouldn't know.

HORACE, JR.: You got a grandfather?

GERTRUDE: No. And I don't have a daddy neither. Your grandfather that just died was a smart man. Did he go to college?

HORACE, JR.: Sure. He went to A & M. He graduated with honors. I had another grandfather, too. He died at thirty-two. A drunkard. He went to college, though. He was a lawyer. What were your grandfathers like?

GERTRUDE: I don't know anything about them.

HORACE, JR.: I know about my daddy's grandfather on his mother's side. And his great-grandfather, he was acting governor of Texas during the war with Mexico. He had two big plantations and one hundred twenty slaves.

GERTRUDE: I'm glad I didn't live then.

HORACE, JR.: Why?

GERTRUDE: Because I wouldn't want to be a slave. Would you?

HORACE, JR.: No. Would you have been a slave?

GERTRUDE: Yes.

HORACE, JR.: Why?

GERTRUDE: Because colored people were the slaves. But no more. And you're not going to do to us what you did to the Indians.

HORACE, JR.: What did we do to the Indians?

GERTRUDE: Killed them all off and moved them onto reservations.

BROTHER (*coming in*): Horace, Jr.

HORACE, JR.: Yes Sir.

BROTHER: Here's a dollar for you.

(*He hands him a dollar.*)

HORACE, JR.: Oh, thank you! (*He takes the dollar and puts it in his pocket.*)

BROTHER: Anybody over here?

HORACE, JR.: Just my big mama and my Aunt Inez.

BROTHER (*taking a swig from a flask*): You won't tell your mama and daddy about my having a drink?

HORACE, JR.: No Sir.

BROTHER: It's been a terrible day for me.

(MR. WILL BORDEN, *a small rancher and farmer, comes in.*)

WILL: Brother, I saw you leave the house and come through the backyard.

BROTHER: Yes Sir, Mr. Will. I snuck over here to have a little drink. Will you join me?

WILL: Thank you.

(*He hands him the flask.* WILL *has a drink.*)

It's a sad day.

BROTHER: Yes Sir.

WILL: Your papa was a good friend to me.

BROTHER: Yes sir.

WILL: I would have gone under twice if it hadn't been for your papa. The goddamn banks had refused to loan me any more. I didn't know where to turn and your papa came to me and he said, "Will, I hear you're in trouble. How much money do you need?" That's the kind of friend he was.

BROTHER: Yes Sir.

WILL: And I want to tell you that if there is any way in this world I can help you or your mother, I want you to call on Mr. Borden.

BROTHER: Yes Sir. I do appreciate that.

(WILL *has another swig from the flask.*)

WILL: What are your plans?

BROTHER: Oh, I don't know, Sir.

WILL: I'd like to see you get into the cattle business. I want to have a talk with you about that one day soon.

BROTHER: Yes Sir.

WILL: There is no one knows more about the cattle business than I do.

BROTHER: No Sir.

WILL (*noticing* GERTRUDE): Who is that?

BROTHER: That's the nurse.

WILL: I tell you . . . let's you and me walk out in the field where we can talk in private. I hear your papa left quite a bit in cash.

BROTHER: Three hundred thousand dollars.

(*They move offstage.* CORELLA *comes out.*)

CORELLA: Come on, Son, now, and get dressed.

HORACE, JR.: Yes Ma'am. (*He goes inside.*)

CORELLA: Gertrude, you come inside and entertain the

baby. I don't want him playing in the dirt now that he's had his bath.

(CORELLA *goes inside.* GERTRUDE *follows.*)

(*The lights fade.*)

(*The lights are brought up down left. It is night.* ELIZABETH *is in her dressing gown.* HORACE, SR., *comes out. He is in his robe.*)

HORACE, SR.: What are you doing up?

ELIZABETH: Sh . . . Don't wake your mother and the children. Go on back to bed. I can't sleep. But you go on back and try to sleep.

(*There is a gentle rapping at the door.* HORACE, SR., *goes.* MRS. VAUGHN *is there. She is still dressed.*)

MRS. VAUGHN: I haven't been able to sleep. I saw your light on over here and so I decided to come see you.

ELIZABETH: Would you like a cup of coffee?

MRS. VAUGHN: No.

ELIZABETH: Haven't you been able to sleep at all?

MRS. VAUGHN: No. Have you?

ELIZABETH: I slept about an hour when I first went to bed.

MRS. VAUGHN: Brother is going to take me out to the cemetery in the morning. Will you go with me?

ELIZABETH: Yes, I will.

MRS. VAUGHN: Will you come with us, big Horace?

HORACE, SR.: All right.

MRS. VAUGHN: They say it was the largest funeral ever held

here. Brother said he was told they had to turn as many away from the church as got in. The funeral procession was over three blocks long. I never saw such flowers, did you?

ELIZABETH: No.

MRS. VAUGHN: I've been thinking about the tombstone. I thought I would have one big stone put in the center of our lot with just the word "Vaughn" on it, and then on his grave I would have the size stone to match the stones on Jenny's and Mary's graves. Does that seem all right to you?

ELIZABETH: Yes Ma'am.

MRS. VAUGHN: The paper asked me for a picture of your papa. You know, the only one I have is just a snapshot. (*She cries.*)

ELIZABETH: Now, Mama. You have to be brave.

MRS. VAUGHN (*wiping her eyes*): Why didn't I make him have a proper picture made? He promised me he would, but you know how he hated doing things like that.

(*She hands her the Kodak picture to look at.* HORACE, JR., *comes out.*)

HORACE, SR.: What are you doing up, Son?

HORACE, JR.: I can't sleep.

HORACE, SR.: Go on back to bed, now.

MRS. VAUGHN: Let him stay up for a little. His grandmother has missed him.

(*She holds out her arms. He goes to her.*)

ELIZABETH: I think this is a fine picture. Don't you, Horace?

(*She shows it to* HORACE, SR.)

HORACE, SR.: I sure do.

MRS. VAUGHN: I hope it can make a proper enlargement. Do you have a picture of your father, big Horace?

HORACE, SR.: No Ma'am. Not a one. Nor of his mother, nor of his father.

MRS. VAUGHN: Did you like Brother Myer's sermon?

ELIZABETH: Yes Ma'am.

MRS. VAUGHN: So did I. Some people didn't think it did your father justice, but I thought it was just fine. I asked for a copy of it. I have a list of everyone that sent flowers or messages. Sis Lucy was heartbroken. She loved Henry so much. He was the right arm of his whole family. (*She gets up.*) It's dawn. I think I'll walk on out to the cemetery.

ELIZABETH: Mama, wait until you have some breakfast.

MRS. VAUGHN: No, I'm so restless. Just be patient with me. I want to go back out there. I feel nearer to him out there.

(*She holds* HORACE, JR., *close to her.*)

(*To* HORACE, JR.:) Will you walk out there with me, Son?

HORACE, JR.: Yes Ma'am.

HORACE, SR.: No. I'll go with you, Mrs. Vaughn.

ELIZABETH: Someone should drive you out.

MRS. VAUGHN: Thank you, but I want to walk. (*She starts away.*)

HORACE, SR.: I have to change my clothes first.

MRS. VAUGHN: All right. I'll wait.

(*He goes.* MRS. VAUGHN *and* ELIZABETH *and* HORACE, JR., *wait in silence.* MRS. VAUGHN *holds* HORACE, JR., *as the lights fade.*)

(*The lights are brought up.* CORELLA *is sitting.* HORACE, JR., *comes in with a book.*)

CORELLA: Hello, Son. Put the book down and talk to me. (*He does so.*) How is school?

HORACE, JR.: All right.

CORELLA: You do well in school, I hear.

(*He grins and shrugs his shoulders.*)

Two years ahead of your class. We're all mighty proud of you. I wish you'd stay outside a little more, though, and not be reading all the time. The fresh air would be good for you. Did your daddy ever tell you about his Uncle Terrence?

HORACE, JR.: I don't think so.

CORELLA: Terrence Robedaux was your daddy's uncle.

HORACE, JR.: Was he your brother?

CORELLA: No. He was Paul Horace's brother. You know who that was, don't you?

HORACE, JR.: That was the name of Daddy's father.

CORELLA: Yes.

HORACE, JR.: He died when Daddy was twelve.

CORELLA: Yes, that's right. Nicotine and alcohol killed him.

HORACE, JR.: I was thinking yesterday during the funeral. My daddy was only a little older than me when his father died. It made me feel funny. I bet he was sad when his father died.

CORELLA: Yes, I guess he was.

HORACE, JR.: Were you sad?

CORELLA: Yes, I was sad. Although I wasn't living with him then. We were separated.

HORACE, JR.: Who was?

CORELLA: We all were. Those were awful times. I love you and that's why I don't want you to ever have to go through times like that. That's why I worry about your reading. You see, one reason your grandfather drank so much was that he had to take care not only of his wife and two small children, but his mother and his sister and her child and his two worthless brothers . . . that just sat around and read books all the time.

HORACE, JR.: Why did he have to take care of them?

CORELLA: Because they couldn't take care of themselves.

HORACE, JR.: Why couldn't they do that?

CORELLA: Because they were all too educated. You see, before the war they owned a shipping fleet in Galveston and they were very rich, but then the Yankees destroyed their fleet and they lost all their money and they were all so educated they couldn't do anything.

HORACE, JR.: I thought he had plantations?

CORELLA: No, honey, that was my grandfather. Your great-grandfather Thornton.

HORACE, JR.: I can't keep them all straight. Papa Vaughn was educated and he was very successful. Mother says he was the most successful man that ever lived here.

CORELLA: That's different. He educated himself. He always had to work.

HORACE, JR.: My daddy has always had to work.

CORELLA: I know he has; too hard, I think sometimes.

(ELIZABETH *and* HORACE, SR., *come in.*)

Can I do anything for you, Elizabeth?

ELIZABETH: No, thank you. I'm all right. I'm going to rest in a little while, if you don't mind seeing to supper.

CORELLA: No. Mary sent over a lot of food left over from the funeral. There is enough in there for three meals.

ELIZABETH: Haven't people been kind?

CORELLA: Yes, they have. Your father was very loved.

ELIZABETH: I know he was.

(*She cries.* HORACE, JR., *goes to her and puts his arms around his mother.*)

Poor Mama. She is grieving so. She wants to go back out to the cemetery again this afternoon.

(MRS. VAUGHN *comes in. She is dressed in black.* CORELLA *gets up and goes to her when she sees her.*)

CORELLA: Oh, Mary, sweet Mary, my old friend . . . I'm so sorry.

MRS. VAUGHN: I know you are. Horace, Jr., you go on run outside and play. I want to talk to your mother and daddy.

(HORACE, JR., *goes out.*)

CORELLA: I'll go see to supper.

MRS. VAUGHN: You don't have to go, Corella. I have no secrets from you.

CORELLA: I know you don't, but I have to get supper started. (*She leaves.*)

MRS. VAUGHN: How long is she staying?

ELIZABETH: She goes back tomorrow.

MRS. VAUGHN (*pause*): Horace, I want your advice about something. I was lying down just now trying to get a little rest, but I couldn't rest at all because my mind was racing, going over and over all I had to get done. (*She cries.*) Oh, my God! Henry tended to everything ever since we were married. I feel so helpless! So very helpless! (*She wipes her eyes.*) But helpless or not, there are decisions to be made. Junior brought me over a copy of his will this afternoon. He left everything to me. I have to go to the office tomorrow or the next day and start going over his books. There is a great deal of money owed him, I know, and I, of course, don't know the first thing about the farms. So, it came to me that I might put Brother in charge of it all. Now, before you comment, hear me out. I know all his weaknesses but I thought that if I showed him my faith in him by turning all my affairs over to him . . . and that . . .

(HORACE, JR., *appears in the yard area with his book and starts to read.*)

way, I pray he would develop a sense of responsibility. He's a bright boy. We all know that. Perhaps he just needs something like this to make him take hold. And so he just doesn't feel he's working for me . . . I'm also going to put the farm out on the Burr Road in his name. I told him what I was going to do just now and he seemed awful pleased. I told him he didn't have to begin work until next week, but he insisted on going down to the office and looking over the books right away. I hope you both approve of what I've done?

HORACE, SR.: I think all that's entirely up to you.

MRS. VAUGHN: How do you feel about it, Elizabeth? Don't you think it might just be the thing to straighten your brother out?

ELIZABETH: I certainly hope so, Mama.

MRS. VAUGHN: Don't you think giving him his own farm was a good idea, Horace? I think it will give him a real sense of responsibility having to make his own decisions. Don't you?

HORACE, SR.: Yes, I think so.

MRS. VAUGHN: I know for a fact your papa, Elizabeth, had two hundred thousand dollars in cash and a fifty thousand dollar life insurance policy. Now, I have to decide how to invest that money. I just don't want it sitting in the bank. I'm thinking of going to the Guardian Trust Company in Houston and letting them invest it for me. What do you think of that?

HORACE, SR.: I think it's a good idea.

MRS. VAUGHN: I don't think either Brother or I know

enough to go on loaning money the way your papa did. Do you?

ELIZABETH: Oh, no. I don't think so either, Mother.

MRS. VAUGHN: That's what I'll do then. Brother will have enough to do collecting the money that's owed the estate and managing the farms and his own farm.

(CORELLA *enters.*)

CORELLA: Can I join you?

ELIZABETH: Come on in.

CORELLA (*going to a chair*): Horace, Jr., is outside reading a book. (*To* MRS. VAUGHN:) It worries me to death the way he reads books. I'm afraid he will turn into another Terrence Robedaux.

MRS. VAUGHN: Mr. Vaughn loved to read, too, you know.

CORELLA: Yes, but he just didn't sit around day and night with a book in his hand. He did lots of other things, too. I mean he was a very successful businessman. Seeing him reading so much worries me to death. Don't it worry you, Horace?

HORACE, SR.: No Ma'am. It doesn't worry me.

(ELIZABETH *goes to the edge of the area.*)

ELIZABETH (*calling*): Horace, Jr., you've read enough today. Go play now.

(*He puts his book down. He goes offstage.* BROTHER *comes in.*)

BROTHER: Hello, Miss Corrie.

CORELLA: Hello, Brother.

(*He goes to his mother and kisses her.*)

MRS. VAUGHN: Hello, Son.

BROTHER: Hello, Sister. Hello, big Horace.

MRS. VAUGHN: I've told Horace and Elizabeth about your new job. They think it's just fine.

BROTHER: Did Mama tell you about the farm she's given me?

ELIZABETH: Yes, she did.

BROTHER: I tell you the first thing I'm going to do is get rid of Leon. I'm going to put a Bohemian out there. Leon is no farmer. He's too old.

MRS. VAUGHN: Now, Son. You can't do that. Leon has been on that place as long as your papa has owned it. It would kill him if you took him off there.

BROTHER: Mama, I'm sorry, but if I'm going to run it, I'm going to run it. I'll put Leon on one of the other farms. I'm going to take half the acreage and put in pecan trees. That's going to be a coming money crop.

(*He turns to* CORELLA.)

How long you gonna be here, Miss Corella?

CORELLA: I leave tomorrow. I just came in for your papa's funeral.

BROTHER (*getting up*): Want me to drive you out to the cemetery this afternoon?

MRS. VAUGHN: Yes, I do.

BROTHER: Then let's get going. I want to go take a look at my farm before dark.

(*She gets up.*)

Will you come with us, Elizabeth?

ELIZABETH: All right. (*To* HORACE, SR.:) Do you want to go?

HORACE, SR.: No. I think I'll stay and visit with Mama.

ELIZABETH: All right. The baby is still taking his nap. Gertrude is with him.

CORELLA: What time do you want supper?

ELIZABETH: We can eat when I get back. How long do you think we'll be, Mama?

MRS. VAUGHN: Not more than an hour.

(*They go out.* HORACE, JR., *is in the yard.*)

Son, you want to go out to the cemetery with us?

HORACE, JR.: All right.

ELIZABETH: Go tell your daddy you're going.

(*He runs inside.*)

HORACE, JR. (*to* HORACE, SR.): I'm going out to the cemetery with Mama.

HORACE, SR.: All right, Son.

(HORACE, JR., *runs off after his mother, grandmother, and uncle.*)

CORELLA: I hope Brother does take hold now. Mary needs him.

(HORACE, SR., *doesn't answer.*)

Your sister and the baby are doing fine now.

HORACE, SR.: That's good.

CORELLA: Will is a good boy and he's making her a good husband.

(*Pause.* HORACE, SR., *seems to have become withdrawn, depressed.*)

How is your business?

HORACE, SR.: It's all right. Kind of quiet this time of the year, though.

CORELLA: You have a lot of responsibility . . . a wife and two children to take care of. (*Pause.*) It would just break my heart if Horace, Jr., turned out like Terrence Robedaux.

(*He gets up. He doesn't answer, but seems even more depressed.*)

Your sister thinks you work too hard. Her husband is a worker, too.

HORACE, SR.: I'm going to feed the chickens.

(HORACE, SR., *goes out as the lights fade.*)

(*The lights are brought up on a section of the Harrison grave-yard.* MRS. VAUGHN, ELIZABETH, HORACE, JR., *and* BROTHER *are there.* BROTHER *has a bucket.* MRS. VAUGHN *has two potted plants.*)

BROTHER: I'm going for water.

(MRS. VAUGHN *takes the plants and gives them to* HORACE, JR.)

MRS. VAUGHN (*to* HORACE, JR.): Go put these on your sister's and your Grandfather Robedaux's graves.

(*The boy takes them and runs off.*)

ELIZABETH: Mother, Brother has been drinking.

MRS. VAUGHN: What?

ELIZABETH: He's been drinking. I can smell it on his breath. Can't you?

MRS. VAUGHN: I don't go around smelling my children's breath.

ELIZABETH: His eyes are all red and bloodshot.

MRS. VAUGHN: Perhaps that comes from grief. After all, he's lost a father that he loved, just like you have. (*She cries.*)

ELIZABETH: I'm sorry, Mother. I didn't say all this to upset you. I'm concerned. You're giving him a lot of responsibility. I just want to be sure that he doesn't start drinking.

MRS. VAUGHN (*wiping her eyes*): We have to have faith in him. If his own mother and sister don't have faith in him, that's part of his trouble. No one has ever had confidence in him. I believe in him. I had hoped . . .

(HORACE, JR., *appears.*)

HORACE, JR.: If my sister had lived she would be twelve years old next month.

ELIZABETH: Yes, she would have.

HORACE, JR.: My Grandfather Robedaux would have been sixty-five. He was thirty-two years old when he died. Daddy is thirty-six. He is four years older than his own father.

(BROTHER *comes in with water. He puts the bucket down.*)

MRS. VAUGHN: I wish I were dead. (*She is sobbing now.*) I wish I had gone instead of your father.

ELIZABETH: No, Mama . . . Please.

MRS. VAUGHN: I do. I do.

(ELIZABETH *holds her mother, comforting her.*)

BROTHER: Don't cry, Mama. Please don't cry. I'm going to take care of you now. I'm going to be the kind of man now Papa always wanted me to be.

MRS. VAUGHN: I know you are, Son. I want you to give me your word, though, you're not going to drink.

BROTHER: I gave you my word about that this afternoon, didn't I? Didn't I swear to you when you gave me the responsibility of the farms I would never drink again? And I meant that, Mama. I am never going to drink again. Little Horace . . .

HORACE, JR.: Yes, Uncle Brother.

BROTHER: I'm going to be a modern farmer. I'm going to plant pecan trees on my farm and I'm going to raise cattle, too. I'm not going to be just dependent on cotton.

MRS. VAUGHN: Cotton was very good to us, Son. Your papa always said the whole county prospered when there was a good cotton crop.

BROTHER: Times are changing, Mama.

MRS. VAUGHN: I guess so.

BROTHER: As a matter of fact, times have changed. Do you

realize all the big fortunes here now are made in leasing land for oil and sulphur? Papa never in all these years had but one little tiny oil lease . . . and the well for that one came in dry . . . Wouldn't it be wonderful now if we got oil wells?

ELIZABETH: I'm content, thank you. I can't see what good oil money has been to any of those that have gotten it.

BROTHER: Horace, Jr., I'm going to buy you a horse. When I get my cattle you and I can ride out to my farm and help see to the cattle. Would you like that?

HORACE, JR.: Yes Sir. My daddy said there was a time not too long ago when everybody rode horses here. And the roads were muddy most of the time. He said sometimes the roads were so muddy even the horses couldn't get through.

BROTHER: Mr. Will Borden is going to advise me about my cattle buying. He and I talked it over and he said he would be very hurt if I didn't let him advise me. He said it would be his privilege to help out Henry Vaughn's son. He said Papa had helped him out a number of times when he had his back against the wall and the banks wouldn't loan him money. He said he would never forget Papa's friendship to him in times of trouble.

MRS. VAUGHN: I can't tell you the number of people that feel that way, that have come to me and said, "If I can help you in any way, let me know, because your husband stood by me when I needed help."

ELIZABETH: Where are you getting the money to buy cattle, Brother?

MRS. VAUGHN: I'm loaning it to him. It's strictly a loan.

Like the bank. He will pay the estate interest like anyone else.

BROTHER: I insisted on that, too.

MRS. VAUGHN: Yes, he did.

HORACE, JR. (*returning from looking at tombstones*): Was my sister that's dead named for this Jenny that's dead?

MRS. VAUGHN: They were both named for my mother, who was a Yerby . . . Jenny Yerby . . .

HORACE, JR.: This Jenny is my aunt. I'm older than she is. I'm older than my own aunt, and daddy is older now than his father. I'm hungry . . .

ELIZABETH: We'll go in a little while.

MRS. VAUGHN: We can go now. I'll come back in the morning.

(*She starts away. The others follow as the lights fade.*)

(*The lights are brought up on the down left living room. HORACE, SR., is there reading one of his newspapers. HORACE, JR., is near him looking at funny papers. There is a pile of newspapers beside him. BROTHER comes in.*)

BROTHER: Everything is getting back to normal. Will you open your store tomorrow?

HORACE, SR.: Yes.

BROTHER: I thought it was foolish keeping it closed on Saturday, seeing as the funeral was on Friday.

HORACE, SR.: I did it out of respect to your papa.

BROTHER: I know you did, and Mama sure did appreciate

it. But I don't think you should have stayed closed on a Saturday, too. After all, Saturday is your busy day.

HORACE, SR.: Things are very quiet now in town. I doubt if I missed out on much being closed.

BROTHER: Are they?

HORACE, SR.: I didn't take in more than a couple of hundred dollars last Saturday.

BROTHER: Is that so? They tell me every store in town was closed during the funeral and over half of them closed Friday all day long.

HORACE, SR.: I'm through reading these newspapers if you want to take them home and look at them. But don't throw them away when you've finished as I've promised them to John Reavis.

BROTHER: Thank you, but I'm too preoccupied to read newspapers. I've got a lot on my mind now. Big Horace, what do you think of Mama turning over her cash to that Houston Trust Company? I went in with her this morning to talk to them and they are so conservative. I've talked to a lot of men around town and they think Mama is foolish. Papa didn't make money by being conservative. He was a plunger. Now, I want you to back me up on this. Mama respects you. I want you to help me get her to let me invest that money. I've already heard of two or three schemes that could double her money in a year . . . Why . . .

HORACE, SR.: Brother, I can't go along with you about this.

BROTHER: What do you mean?

HORACE, SR.: I can't. That's what I mean. I have to tell you right now, if your mother asks my opinion I would have to tell her that I would give the money to the Houston Investment Company.

BROTHER: That's why you'll never have a dime.

HORACE, SR.: Maybe so.

BROTHER: Papa always said you'd never have anything because you had no vision and no imagination. You were a plodder. Honest and trustworthy, but not smart . . . What the hell do you know about it, anyway?

HORACE, SR.: Then why did you ask my opinion?

BROTHER: I don't know.

HORACE, SR.: Don't anymore, because this is one thing I want to keep out of.

BROTHER: Well, just see you do. And don't be offering Mama any free advice.

HORACE, SR.: I don't think I do that.

BROTHER: Well, don't.

(ELIZABETH *comes in.* HORACE, SR., *goes back to his paper.*)

HORACE, JR.: When do I get my horse?

BROTHER (*getting up*): I don't know. (*He goes out.*)

ELIZABETH: What's the matter with him?

HORACE, SR.: He got mad at me because I won't tell your mama to let him invest her money instead of giving it to the trust company to handle.

ELIZABETH: Oh, my God! That's all Mama needs!

HORACE, JR.: I smelled liquor on his breath and I saw him

out in the backyard just before coming into the house taking a swig from a flask.

ELIZABETH: Now, you be quiet. That's none of your business. Do you hear me?

HORACE, JR.: Yes Ma'am.

HORACE, SR.: Do you think I'm a plodder and unimaginative?

ELIZABETH: No. I certainly don't. Why?

HORACE, SR.: Brother said that was your papa's opinion of me.

ELIZABETH: If it was, I never heard it.

MRS. VAUGHN (*coming in*): I have to make a decision about the Houston Trust Company. Brother thinks we can do more with the money by investing it ourselves. What do you think, Horace?

HORACE, SR.: I have no opinion about it.

ELIZABETH: Yes, you have, Horace. Tell her what it is.

HORACE, SR.: No, Elizabeth. It's no business of mine. (*He leaves.*)

ELIZABETH: He's against it.

MRS. VAUGHN: Why?

ELIZABETH: Because he doesn't think Brother knows enough to handle it wisely.

MRS. VAUGHN: Well, that's his opinion. Isn't it?

ELIZABETH: It's not yours?

MRS. VAUGHN: No. It's not, Elizabeth. I have been very impressed with the way your brother has gone into my affairs. Very impressed.

ELIZABETH: Very well.

MRS. VAUGHN: Henry always thought Horace, Sr., was a plodder. Much too conservative.

ELIZABETH: He also thought, at one time, he was a gambler and a wastrel and would never have any sense of responsibility and so did you, if I remember correctly.

MRS. VAUGHN: For heaven's sakes, Elizabeth. That's the past. I had no idea you still held that against me. I thought you had forgiven us for that.

ELIZABETH: I have.

MRS. VAUGHN: You don't sound like it.

ELIZABETH: I just don't care for your disparaging remarks about Horace. That's all.

MRS. VAUGHN: I'll never discuss him with you again. You can be assured.

(*They sit in silence.*)

HORACE, JR.: Are you mad at each other?

ELIZABETH: No, we're not mad at each other.

HORACE, JR.: Well, you act like it. (*Pause.*) Why didn't you and Papa want Mother and Daddy to get married?

ELIZABETH: You be quiet now. You're getting too big for your breeches. Where did you hear about that?

HORACE, JR.: I heard Miss Ida talking one day. She said

you and Daddy had to elope because Papa and Grandma didn't want you to marry him.

MRS. VAUGHN: Well, we were wrong.

HORACE, JR.: Miss Ida said it was on Valentine's Day.

ELIZABETH: Yes, it was. It was eleven years ago last Valentine's Day.

MRS. VAUGHN: March is the month I'll never forget.

HORACE, JR.: Why?

MRS. VAUGHN: Because this is March. Your Papa died in March.

HORACE, JR.: And it's my birthday, too.

MRS. VAUGHN: Of course it is, forgive me.

(*She holds him.*)

Grief makes us so selfish. Forgive your grandmother. The day you were born was a very happy time for us all.

(*She holds him.*)

(*The lights fade.*)

Act Two

The lights are brought up on the area up left. MRS. VAUGHN *is writing letters.* ELIZA *comes in with her brother,* WALTER.

ELIZA: This is my brother, Walter.

(MRS. VAUGHN *looks up from her letters.*)

MRS. VAUGHN: Hello, Walter.

WALTER: Howdy do.

MRS. VAUGHN: Did Eliza tell you what I want you for?

WALTER: Yes Ma'am.

MRS. VAUGHN: Are you a good driver?

WALTER: Yes Ma'am.

MRS. VAUGHN: And you can help around the yard?

WALTER: Yes Ma'am.

MRS. VAUGHN: Very good. My son is anxious for me to learn to drive but I don't care to. Your main duty will be to drive me to the cemetery every afternoon, and sometimes in the morning. My son used to take me, but he's very busy now. He planted a hundred pecan trees on his farm. He also has bought himself a herd of cattle. They are putting up proper fencing now, as the cattle are to be brought in next week. You'll live in the house next to Eliza's and Sarah's.

WALTER: Yes Ma'am.

MRS. VAUGHN: Seven dollars a week salary. Is that all right?

WALTER: Yes Ma'am.

MRS. VAUGHN: Have you chauffeured before?

WALTER: For Mrs. Rogers.

ELIZA: He was in the war.

MRS. VAUGHN: I know, you told me. You went to France, didn't you?

WALTER: Yes Ma'am.

MRS. VAUGHN: You weren't wounded, I hope?

WALTER: No Ma'am.

ELIZA: He crossed the ocean on a boat. He weren't seasick, either.

HORACE, JR.: Gertrude says you saw a mermaid in the ocean.

WALTER: I sure did. I saw four.

HORACE, JR.: And Gertrude says you've got second sight.

ELIZA: We all have in my family except Gertrude.

WALTER: My daddy is a preacher.

HORACE, JR.: Gertrude says you saw a fiery chariot in the middle of the road on the way to church.

MRS. VAUGHN: All right, Horace, Jr. Don't waste Walter's time. You can start in today, Walter, if you want to.

(*She goes back to her letter writing.* WALTER *and* ELIZA *leave followed by* HORACE, JR.)

HORACE, JR. (*to* WALTER): Tell me about the fiery chariot.

WALTER: We were driving in the buggy to church last Sunday and we got near the Peach Creek Bridge and the horses started pitching and neighing and Lorenzo couldn't make them go. The more he whipped them the more stubborn they got. Finally I said: "Lorenzo, stop whipping them horses; they will never cross that fiery chariot." "What fiery chariot?", he said. "The one there in the road. Can't you see it?" "No," he said.

HORACE, JR. (*to* ELIZA): Could you see it?

ELIZA: I was here cooking last Sunday . . . if I had been along, though, I could have seen it.

HORACE, JR.: Did they shoot at you in France?

WALTER: They sure did.

ELIZA: They didn't touch him, though. Our brother, Buddy, got killt. The second day he was there. I knew the minute he was killt. (*She puts her hand to her heart.*) It was just like something hit me here. I said to my sister, I said: "Buddy's been killt . . . send for Papa."

HORACE, JR.: She seen two doves up there the day my papa died.

(BROTHER *comes in.* ELIZA *goes.*)

BROTHER: Horace, Jr., go look in the barn. There is a surprise for you there.

(HORACE, JR., *goes running off.*)

I bought him a horse. He doesn't know a thing about one. Will you help him saddle it, Walter?

WALTER: Yes Sir.

(*He goes.* BROTHER *looks around to see if he's being watched, decides he isn't, and takes out a flask and has a drink for himself.* ELIZA *comes back in.*)

ELIZA: Your mother says Mr. Will Borden called from town. He wants to see you in your office.

BROTHER: Thank you.

(*He leaves.* ELIZA *goes as the lights fade.*)

(*The lights are brought up on the Vaughn family plot.* WALTER, MRS. VAUGHN, ELIZABETH, *and* HORACE, JR., *come in.*)

MRS. VAUGHN: Do you like the tombstone?

ELIZABETH: Oh, yes, I do. I think it looks wonderful, Mama.

MRS. VAUGHN: So do I. I'm very pleased. Do you like it, Walter?

WALTER: Yes'm.

MRS. VAUGHN: I'm going to have a stained-glass window put in the new church in his memory.

ELIZABETH: That's lovely.

MRS. VAUGHN: It will cost me a thousand dollars.

ELIZABETH: It's worth it.

MRS. VAUGHN: I think so. Of course, he never would join the church, but he went every Sunday anyway.

ELIZABETH: Was he always a Methodist?

MRS. VAUGHN: His family was. I was a Presbyterian, but when I came here there was no Presbyterian Church and I started going to the Methodist Church and after we married, I joined. (*Pause.*) I remember when little Jenny died. Your papa was sitting in the living room beside her body and Mrs. Coon Ferguson came in and she said, "Mr. Vaughn, did you ever think God did this to you because you don't belong to the church?" Your papa turned beet red and finally he said just quietly . . . "No, Mrs. Ferguson, I never did."

(*She looks at* HORACE, JR.)

Why are you so quiet, Son? You aren't sick, are you?

ELIZABETH: He's mad because I made him stop riding that horse for a while. That's all he wants to do now, morning, noon, and night.

MRS. VAUGHN: I don't think I'm going to plant a lot of shrubs and flowers out here. I think I'm just going to keep it simple.

ELIZABETH: I would.

MRS. VAUGHN: Do you realize he's been gone four months? I haven't been out to visit the farms once since his death. I'm going to start going. Walter, do you know where our farms are?

WALTER: Yes Ma'am. I do.

MRS. VAUGHN: I'm glad you do, because I don't.

(WALTER *walks to another part of the cemetery.*)

Elizabeth, I want to do something for you and big Horace. I've done so much for Brother.

ELIZABETH: We have all we need, Mama. You and Papa gave me the piano and the house.

MRS. VAUGHN: Let me get you a car. I hate to see Horace walking to town every day in this sun.

ELIZABETH: We don't need a car, Mama.

(*Pause.*)

MRS. VAUGHN: Now, look, I know he's worried to death about his business. I know his business has not been good.

ELIZABETH: Now, Mother . . .

MRS. VAUGHN: I have eyes. I can see the poor man is worrying himself to death. I want to give him some money to tide him over.

ELIZABETH: Now, Mama, you know that's out of the question. He'll never take it from you.

MRS. VAUGHN: Then let me give it to you and you can give it to him. (*Pause.*) Please, Elizabeth. I want to help. What good is money if you can't help your children?

(ELIZABETH *doesn't answer.* WALTER *comes back.*)

I'm ready to go now, if you all are.

(WALTER *starts out.* ELIZABETH, HORACE, JR., *and* MRS. VAUGHN *follow as the lights fade.*)

(*The lights are brought up downstage left.* ELIZABETH *and* HORACE, JR., *come in.*)

HORACE, JR.: Why does Daddy need money?

ELIZABETH: He just does.

HORACE, JR.: I heard him say the other night he had been worried about money all his life. Why is that?

ELIZABETH: He's just worried is all.

HORACE, JR.: Do we have enough to eat?

ELIZABETH: Yes, we do. Now, you know we do.

HORACE, JR.: Do you think he will lose his store?

ELIZABETH: Why would you think that?

HORACE, JR.: I heard him talking to you. He said he owed the bank so much money he was afraid they wouldn't loan him any more and he'd lose everything.

ELIZABETH: Don't you ever repeat that to anyone. Do you hear me?

HORACE, JR.: Daddy works hard.

ELIZABETH: Yes, he does.

HORACE, JR.: Aren't you supposed to have money when you work hard?

ELIZABETH: I think you are.

HORACE, JR.: Why doesn't he?

ELIZABETH: I don't know. His business depends on the cotton crop and the cotton crop hasn't done well lately.

HORACE, JR.: Does everybody around here depend upon the cotton crop?

ELIZABETH: More or less.

HORACE, JR.: Is everybody poor?

ELIZABETH: No, I can't say that.

HORACE, JR.: Why is that?

ELIZABETH: I can't explain it; it's just how things are.

HORACE, JR.: Does everybody owe money at the bank?

ELIZABETH: No.

HORACE, JR.: Is Grandma poor?

ELIZABETH: No, you know she's not.

HORACE, JR.: Is she rich?

ELIZABETH: In a way.

HORACE, JR.: Is she the richest person here?

ELIZABETH: Oh, no. Not by any means.

HORACE, JR.: Is Gertrude poor?

ELIZABETH: Yes.

HORACE, JR.: Why?

ELIZABETH: Because she hasn't any money.

HORACE, JR.: Does her mother have money?

ELIZABETH: No.

HORACE, JR.: Why?

ELIZABETH: Because she doesn't get paid much.

HORACE, JR.: She works hard?

ELIZABETH: Yes.

HORACE, JR.: Why doesn't she get paid then?

ELIZABETH: Because that's how things are.

HORACE, JR.: Did you ever work?

ELIZABETH: Yes. I taught piano.

HORACE, JR.: Did you get paid very much?

ELIZABETH: No. Not too much.

HORACE, JR.: Is Eliza Gertrude's mother?

ELIZABETH: No, her aunt. And Walter is her uncle.

HORACE, JR.: Gertrude said she would like to be a nurse or a teacher someday to help her race.

ELIZABETH: Did she?

HORACE, JR.: I'd like to help my race, too. What can I do?

ELIZABETH: Well, I don't know. We'll have to think about it. Start by being a good man; that will help all the races.

HORACE, JR.: How do I be a good man?

ELIZABETH: God only knows, honey.

HORACE, JR.: Is Daddy a good man?

ELIZABETH: I think so. I know he tries to be.

HORACE, JR.: Was Papa?

ELIZABETH: Oh, yes. Very good!

HORACE, JR.: Why?

ELIZABETH: Because he was.

HORACE, JR.: Was Daddy's father . . . Mister Paul Horace?

ELIZABETH: Don't call him Mister, honey, he's your grand-father, too.

HORACE, JR.: What should I call him?

ELIZABETH: Grandfather.

HORACE, JR.: Will I ever see him?

ELIZABETH: I expect so, some day.

HORACE, JR.: When?

ELIZABETH: In heaven.

HORACE, JR.: He drank whiskey and smoked cigarettes. I don't think you get to heaven if you do that.

ELIZABETH: Who told you that?

HORACE, JR.: I heard Miss Ida say it. She said God wouldn't have you if you did that.

ELIZABETH: Who did she say that to?

HORACE, JR.: Her boy.

ELIZABETH: Well, I don't believe that.

HORACE, JR.: You mean I can smoke and drink and still go to heaven?

ELIZABETH: Oh, honey, I don't know really what gets us to heaven or keeps us away.

HORACE, JR.: Uncle Brother drinks and smokes.

ELIZABETH: I know.

HORACE, JR.: Is he going to heaven?

ELIZABETH: I hope so.

HORACE, JR.: If I see Daddy's papa in heaven, how am I going to know him? I have never seen a picture of him.

ELIZABETH: Oh, I don't know, honey.

HORACE, JR.: How will he know me? He's never seen a picture of me either.

ELIZABETH: What?

HORACE, JR.: I said . . . (*Pause.*) You aren't half listening to me.

ELIZABETH: Yes, I am.

HORACE, JR.: Are you worried?

ELIZABETH: No.

HORACE, JR.: Where's Henry Vaughn?

ELIZABETH: He's out riding with your grandmother. They went out to the farms. (*Pause.*) Son, Mother is going to have another baby.

HORACE, JR.: Are you? When?

ELIZABETH: In six months.

HORACE, JR.: Is it going to be a boy or a girl?

ELIZABETH: I don't know. You can't ever know that.

HORACE, JR.: What do you want?

ELIZABETH: I'd like a girl, since I have two boys.

HORACE, JR.: You have a girl, too. She is dead, but you have her. What happens to you when you die?

ELIZABETH: I don't know.

HORACE, JR.: Do you change?

ELIZABETH: Honey, I just don't know.

HORACE, JR.: Suppose I die . . .

ELIZABETH: You're not going to die.

HORACE, JR.: Why? Could you keep me from it?

(HORACE, SR., *comes in. He has a bag of groceries. He takes a package out of the bag of groceries and gives it to* HORACE, JR.)

HORACE, SR. (*to* HORACE, JR.): Go feed the cats for me.

(*He takes the package and goes off.*)

ELIZABETH: He asks so many questions. I've never known a more inquisitive child. We have to be careful how we talk around him, too. He hears everything we say. (*Pause.*) How was business?

HORACE, SR.: Terrible. One of the worst days I've ever had. There is just no money at all in the county. I don't know what people are going to do.

ELIZABETH: Maybe they'll make a crop this year.

HORACE, SR.: If they do, there's no price for it at all. Just none. You can't make a living on twelve-cent cotton. (*Pause.*) I'm going to have to go to the bank tomorrow and ask them to extend my loan. I hate like the devil to do it, but I just have to see if they will carry me a little longer.

ELIZABETH: I'm sure they will. You've always paid them so promptly.

HORACE, SR.: Don't be too sure. They have a lot of notes

now they're not collecting. No one can pay their notes these days.

ELIZABETH: What if they won't extend your note?

HORACE, SR.: Then they'll close my store and take my stock.

ELIZABETH: Would you have to go bankrupt?

HORACE, SR.: No, I don't believe in doing that. I'd just have to get a job somehow and pay off what I owe them.

ELIZABETH: Mama wants to give me some money. We could use that to pay off the bank.

HORACE, SR.: That's your money. I don't want that.

ELIZABETH: Why are you like that? Why can't you ever accept help?

HORACE, SR.: Because I want to work this out myself. (*Pause.*) Besides, your mother had better watch how she gives her money away. She's liable to wind up with nothing. Brother was uptown today drunk as a loon. He's spending money like a crazy man. He's not tending to her business at all. And he's certainly not seeing to his own farm. (*Pause.*) I'm going to tell you something that I heard today. I don't want to worry you, but . . .

(HORACE, JR., *comes in.*)

HORACE, JR.: The cats are all fed.

ELIZABETH: I told Horace, Jr., about the baby.

HORACE, JR.: What do you want . . . a boy or a girl?

HORACE, SR.: I've never cared. Run along, Son, I'm talking to your mother.

HORACE, JR.: Can't I hear?

HORACE, SR.: No, now run on. Have you fed and watered your horse for the night?

HORACE, JR.: No Sir.

HORACE, SR.: Then go do it.

(*He goes.*)

(*To* ELIZABETH:) I heard uptown today that your brother had heavily mortgaged the farm your mother gave him.

ELIZABETH: What for?

HORACE, SR.: God knows.

ELIZABETH: She gave him money to buy the cattle and the pecan trees.

HORACE, SR.: I know. But he's living high. He has a new car and he goes to Houston three or four nights a week. I think he has a woman there.

ELIZABETH: Oh, my God! Poor Mama!

(BROTHER *comes in. He is quite drunk.*)

BROTHER: Where's Mama?

ELIZABETH: Walter drove her out to the farms.

BROTHER: What the hell is she going to the farms for? She doesn't know anything about the damn farms.

ELIZABETH: Maybe she should learn. They're her farms.

BROTHER: She can have them. She'll come back depressed, let me tell you. The crops look terrible. If I had my way, I'd get all new tenants. We haven't got a farmer on a single place of ours. Not one.

HORACE, SR.: No one is making crops here. You can't blame the farmers.

BROTHER: I blame these. All they do is complain. And they always want something. Mr. Brother, give us this. Mr. Brother, give us that. Give us. Give us that . . . My God! They're all helpless. They can't do a damn thing for themselves. Give me this. Give me that. My God! (*He looks at his sister.*) What's the matter with you? You look in a sour mood.

ELIZABETH: You're drunk. My God, Brother! Don't you ever learn? Don't your promises mean anything? Mama is going to have an attack of asthma when she sees you this way. How dare you come home this way? In this condition? You know you have responsibilities now. You are managing a large estate. You are managing farms and money that belongs to your mother. What kind of impression does it make for people to see you walking the streets drunk? (*Pause.*) I'm sorry. Forgive me for lashing out this way. It's none of my business. This is between you and Mama.

BROTHER: No. No. No. You're right. You are perfectly right. The ghost of Papa is heavy on me. I get so sick of people saying, "I know you're going to turn into a fine man like your papa. Henry Vaughn's son couldn't help but be a fine businessman. Smart . . . successful . . ." I'm not smart. I never have been. I'm dumb. I'm stupid. I've no judgement.

ELIZABETH: That's ridiculous. You are certainly smart enough . . .

BROTHER: And I've no luck. I never have had. I never will have. Look at Papa. Everything he touched turned out well. Everything . . . But for me? Nothing works out . . . Nothing . . . (*He takes a flask of whiskey. He has a swig.*) You can't believe what I had to pay for this. You know where I bought it? Not out in the country from some Bohemian. Right here in town. Harvey Douglas is making it. Not very good, though. Bohemians make it best.

ELIZABETH: You're going to kill yourself drinking that bootleg stuff.

BROTHER: I don't get drunk every day, you know. Not every day. I had bad news today. I have reason to be drunk. I had very bad news. (*He sighs.*) Oh, Jesus! That's all I ever have is bad news. The Bohemians on my place came in this morning to tell me that half the pecan trees I planted have died and the other half look very sickly.

ELIZABETH: Did you go out and look at the trees?

BROTHER: Not yet. I've been too depressed to go.

ELIZABETH: Well, I'd certainly go out there and look at them for myself.

HORACE, SR.: If they were my trees I'd get the county agent out there and see if anything can be done.

ELIZABETH: I certainly wouldn't sit around and drink and feel sorry for myself.

BROTHER: Oh, you wouldn't.

ELIZABETH: No. I wouldn't.

BROTHER: That's because you've never known trouble. You had a mother and father always take care of you and now you have a husband: you've never had any worries or any responsibilities.

ELIZABETH: Oh, no.

MRS. VAUGHN (*coming in*): Brother, I have just come from the farms. They are a mess. A terrible mess. I have never seen them in such a deplorable condition.

BROTHER: What the hell do you know about them? You stay away from there.

MRS. VAUGHN: They are my farms. I will certainly not stay away from them.

BROTHER: Then take them over. I'll be happy if you do. I'm sick of them. Absolutely sick of them. I'd like to see you do something with them. You think it is so easy? They're stupid, every one of those tenants. Lazy and stupid. All I hear is, your papa didn't do it this way. Your papa didn't do it that way. I'm sick to death of hearing about how Papa did things. Was he so perfect? Was he some kind of god? I didn't think he was so damn perfect. I thought he made plenty of mistakes. Plenty. I was scared as hell of him, for one thing. He always made me feel like I couldn't do anything. I was dumb . . . I was incompetent.

MRS. VAUGHN: And you're drunk.

BROTHER: Yes, I am. God damn it! I am. I've been drunk all day, but I know what I'm saying. And if Papa were here, I'd tell him. I'm not Papa. I'm never going to be Papa. I don't want to be him, or like him in any way . . . Not in any way. (*Pause.*) I'm sorry. Forgive me, Mama. There's a devil in me. I don't know why I say things like that. Please, forget I said those things. Please, please. Everything has gone wrong today. The pecan trees on my farm are not doing well, half have died . . . and I don't know how to get the tenants to do anything at all. I admit that. Nothing at all. But I'm going to learn to stand up to them. I know that's what they want. Mr. Thatcher came to me right after Papa died and he knew I was to take over. He said, "Let me tell you your papa's method. He was always fair with the tenants but he was firm. His word was law. Once he gave an order, he saw that it was carried out to the letter." And I know he did that; and that's what I haven't learned to do yet, because they always say your papa didn't want it done that way . . . he wanted it done this way . . . your papa . . . (*Pause.*) And I get troubled then and I think maybe they're right. Maybe Papa wants it done this way and I think . . .

GERTRUDE (*coming in*): Mr. Horace, little Horace said to tell you he can't get the horse into the barn.

HORACE, SR.: Where is he?

GERTRUDE: He's in the pasture. Still can't catch him.

(HORACE, SR., *goes out.* GERTRUDE *follows after him.*)

MRS. VAUGHN: I'm sorry to hear you were afraid of your father. I'm glad he never knew that. It would have been very distressing to him. (*Pause.*) Eliza has your supper ready. It's on the table.

BROTHER: Have you eaten?

MRS. VAUGHN: No. I can't eat, thank you. I'm too upset to eat. I'll have some tea or milk toast later.

(BROTHER *goes.*)

In three months I have never in my life seen farms deteriorate so.

ELIZABETH: Horace seems to think all the farms in the county are being neglected because the farmers are so discouraged about prices and weather conditions.

(HORACE, SR., *comes back in.*)

MRS. VAUGHN: You can't see the cotton for the Johnson grass in most places. The cotton is literally being choked out. There was not a soul working in the fields in any place. All they do is complain about Brother. They say he never comes out, that he never gives them what they ask for or need. (*Pause.*) Horace, I know you have your own troubles, but will you let Walter drive you out to the farms on Sunday and see what you advise my doing? Maybe they are just using Mr. Vaughn's death as an excuse and if they are, of course . . . but then . . . maybe they're not . . .

BROTHER (*coming back in*): I've come back to apologize to you all. To take back everything I said. I worshiped my father. He was a great and good man and if you want to know why I drink, it is because I know that I can never in any way live up to him. Not in any way be worthy of him. Nobody can. Nobody ever in this world. (*Pause.*) But, I tell you this. I am going to try from now on to be like him in every way I can. Beginning tomorrow morning I'm going to be up at four-thirty and I'm going out to those farms every day. And I'm going to get them straightened out if it means working in the fields myself. (*Pause.*) Mama, I'm desperate. I have to tell you everything. I went crazy. I lost my reason. I borrowed money on the farm you gave me from the bank and I spent that and I went to get more and they wouldn't loan it to me, so I went to John Carson and he loaned me money but he is charging me twenty-five percent interest on it. I'm not making my payments because I'm so in debt everywhere and he is threatening to take the farm from me and the cattle and, my God! . . . I wish I were dead!

MRS. VAUGHN: Don't say that!

BROTHER: I do. I am a failure. A complete, total failure and I would be better off dead. I wish I were out in that graveyard instead of Papa. Why would God take a fine man like that and leave here to suffer a no-good weakling like me? Why, Mama? Why?

MRS. VAUGHN (*holding him to her*): Don't talk that way. Please.

BROTHER: Why? Why? Why?

MRS. VAUGHN: Sh . . . Sh . . . We'll find a way out of all this. Yes, we will.

HORACE, JR. (*coming in*): I fed the horse.

ELIZABETH: Run on, Son.

HORACE, JR.: I want my supper.

ELIZABETH: Gertrude has it for you.

(*He leaves.* BROTHER *is crying.* MRS. VAUGHN *comforts him. He leaves.*)

MRS. VAUGHN: Poor thing. Why is he always in such trouble? Why? Horace, will you call up John Carson for me and ask him how much Brother owes him?

(*Pause.*)

HORACE, SR.: Yes Ma'am.

MRS. VAUGHN: Tell him I'll pay him back right away. (*Pause.*) I know what you're both saying . . . Let him get out of this himself. And the next time I will, I swear to you. But I can't let him lose that farm. That was one of your papa's favorites. One of his very favorites. (*She goes.*)

HORACE, SR.: You see what I'm telling you? He's going to break her. She'll wind up with nothing. Not one penny. And I tell you something else. Horace, Jr., is going to have to start taking more responsibility around this place or he's going to end up just like your brother. I was working at his age and on my own at twelve. I want him to start working in the store with me on Saturdays. He can take clothes to the tailor for me and go to the bank for change and sweep out in the morning. And he can . . . (*Pause.*) What the hell am I talking about? Your brother worked. He worked all the time as a boy, and look at him.

(ELIZABETH *is crying.*)

I'm sorry. I shouldn't talk about him this way. It's insensitive of me.

(*She wipes her eyes.*)

ELIZABETH: I feel so for him. What is going to happen to him? (*Pause.*) I know this. I feel this . . . (*Pause.*) Oh, I don't know anything, really. I was about to say Mama and Papa made a mistake getting him out of his scrapes, but there are other boys whose parents have done that and they have recovered and made good men.

GERTRUDE (*coming in*): Henry Vaughn is in bed. He says will you come read him a story?

ELIZABETH: All right.

(*She goes.* HORACE, SR., *gets a newspaper and sits and begins reading.* HORACE, JR., *comes in.*)

HORACE, JR.: What are you reading?

HORACE, SR.: One of my out-of-town papers.

HORACE, JR.: Which one?

HORACE, SR.: *Kansas City Star.* (*Pause.*) I want you to come to work with me at the store next Saturday.

HORACE, JR.: Yes Sir.

HORACE, SR.: And maybe you can start bringing me my dinner from here at noontime. I get so tired of eating in town.

HORACE, JR.: Yes Sir. You ought to have a clerk so you can come home for dinner.

HORACE, SR.: I can't afford a clerk with business the way it is. (*He takes an envelope out of his pocket.*) Look here. This came today.

(*He takes a photograph out of his pocket and hands it to the boy.*)

HORACE, JR.: Who is that?

HORACE, SR.: My father. Your grandfather. I wrote an uncle of mine. I told him I didn't have a picture to show you and he sent me this one. (*He studies it.*) I don't know how old he was then. To tell you the truth, I don't remember his looking like this at all. He looks like he's in his early twenties. He looks younger than I do, doesn't he?

HORACE, JR.: Yes Sir.

HORACE, SR.: My memory of him was that he had a mustache and he had reddish hair. He was a small, thin man. To tell you the truth, whenever I think of him, I think of him like he was when he was so sick. He was so thin and he coughed a lot. I wanted to go visit him, but I was almost afraid to go, because I knew how sick he was. (*Pause.*) I have his watch in the safe at the store. When you're twenty-one I'm going to get it fixed and give it to you.

HORACE, JR.: Who is that lady with him?

HORACE, SR.: That's my mother.

HORACE, JR.: She's pretty.

HORACE, SR.: Yes, she was.

HORACE, JR.: Were you born then?

HORACE, SR.: I don't know. I doubt it.

HORACE, JR.: She worries about me.

HORACE, SR.: Who does? Mama?

HORACE, JR.: Yes Sir. She thinks I read too much.

HORACE, SR.: Well, I don't worry about you. I'm going to stand by you in any way I can and I'm going to see you get an education if you want one. I don't want you ever to have to scratch around the way I have. I tell you, a man without an education today is at a great disadvantage. You realize next year you'll be in the sixth grade and that was the grade I was in when I quit?

ELIZABETH (*coming in*): Mama called. She wanted to know if you'd called John Carson about Brother's debt.

HORACE, SR.: I'll go by his store tomorrow. I don't want to ask him something like that on the telephone. Half the town knows what you say over the telephone.

HORACE, JR.: This is a picture of my grandfather.

ELIZABETH (*looking at it*): This is Miss Corrie with him, isn't it?

HORACE, SR.: Yes.

ELIZABETH: You know, I don't remember your father at all.

HORACE, SR.: How could you? You were only six when he died.

ELIZABETH: I've never seen a picture of him before. You don't look a thing like him.

HORACE, SR.: No. I look like my mother's people.

(BROTHER *comes in. He is sobering now; he looks very tired.*)

BROTHER: Have you called John Carson?

HORACE, SR.: No.

BROTHER: You don't have to call him. I know to the penny what I owe him.

HORACE, SR.: What about the interest?

BROTHER: That, too.

(*He hands him some figures.*)

Here . . .

(HORACE, SR., *looks at it.*)

Mama is taking the farm back. She's paying John Carson

and the bank back and putting the farm back in her name. I don't blame her. I swear to you, I don't. I just don't know how to manage money. Mama said, "Where did you spend all this money? On what?" On nothing. I spent it absolutely on nothing. I haven't anything to show for it.

HORACE, SR.: What is to become of your cattle?

BROTHER: Mama says I can use the land for them, but to tell you the truth, I want to sell them. I want to clear out of here. I've known nothing but failure here. Do you remember the time I went to Germany on the boat? I liked that. I like traveling. I think I would like to be a merchant seaman.

ELIZABETH: Have you told this to Mama?

BROTHER: No. None of it. But I will tell her. I can always sign up on a ship out of Galveston. I'd like to go around the world.

ELIZABETH: Oh, Brother, I hate to see you go so far away from us. I wish you could meet a nice girl and settle down and have a family.

GERTRUDE (*coming in*): I'm going home now.

ELIZABETH: All right. Thank you, Gertrude. Will I see you tomorrow?

GERTRUDE: No Ma'am. I'm going fishing tomorrow.

HORACE, SR.: Where are you fishing?

GERTRUDE: We're fishing at the mouth of Caney Creek. If I catch anything, I'll bring you some fish for your supper.

HORACE, SR.: Thank you.

(*She goes.*)

I used to love to fish.

BROTHER (*to* HORACE, JR.): Your daddy used to make his living selling fish when he was about your age.

HORACE, JR.: I know.

ELIZABETH: Poor boy, he's heard it enough. He's sick of hearing about it, I'm sure. (*Pause.*) Won't you miss your friends, Brother?

BROTHER: What friends? Mr. Will Borden cheated me, you know, on the cattle. He swindled me. I could have done better with any stranger. But I trusted him.

ELIZABETH: Oh, Brother . . .

BROTHER: It's true. I was told yesterday that I paid twice as much for the cattle as I should have. Exactly twice as much.

ELIZABETH: Are you sure?

BROTHER: I had three reputable men tell me. All at different times.

WALTER (*coming over*): Miss Elizabeth . . . Eliza says somebody better come see to your mama. She's having a terrible asthma attack.

ELIZABETH: All right. I'll be right over.

(WALTER *goes.*)

Brother, I wouldn't let Mr. Will Borden get by with something like that. The old hypocrite! He was always telling us what a friend Papa had been to him and how he would never forget it and would do everything in his power to repay him.

BROTHER: I know. I know. Why, to hear the town talk after he died, you would think everyone here was his dearest and closest friend. Why, you couldn't walk down the street for people stopping you and telling you how much they thought of him. How much he had done for them . . . how indebted they felt to him. They were going to name streets for him. Why, there was even talk of a monument, and now . . . those same people, those same friends cross the other side of the street when they see me coming.

ELIZABETH: Oh . . . they don't, Brother. You're just sensitive.

BROTHER: Oh, yes, they do! And where are the monuments, and what streets have been named for him?

HORACE, JR.: My other grandmother said he had the largest funeral ever known here. Did he?

ELIZABETH: I think so, honey.

HORACE, JR.: Eliza said she saw two mourning doves on the house the morning he died. Do mourning doves always come when you're going to die?

ELIZABETH: That's just a superstition, honey.

HORACE, JR.: I saw a mourning dove in our yard today and I took a rock and I chucked it at him. I chased it away. It lit on Miss Ida's pear tree. But it didn't go on her house.

ELIZABETH: Does Mama know about Mr. Will Borden?

BROTHER: Yes. She went to the phone and tried to reach him, but his son said he'd gone out for the evening.

ELIZABETH: I'd better go on over to her. (*She leaves.*)

BROTHER: You owe the bank money?

HORACE, SR.: Yes, I do.

BROTHER: God help you, then. They're a cold-blooded bunch over there, too. And you know Papa saved that bank. Back about fifteen years ago they were having crop failures like they are now and the bank had loaned too much money and wasn't able to collect any of it. Everyone was turning in their farms and they couldn't resell them and they were about to go under when Papa went over with fifty thousand dollars and let them have it to use with no interest so they could keep their doors open. That's the kind of man he was. And, of course, they vowed they would never forget it. But have any of them remembered? They treat me like anybody else. I'm Papa's son. And they treat me like any other customer. Well, to hell with them! When you're on a boat no one knows who you are or where you came from and no one cares.

ELIZABETH (*coming back*): Mama was asleep by the time I got there. Her breathing sounded normal enough. Eliza said she'd sleep in her room tonight and if she gets any worse, she'll call me.

HORACE, SR.: It's close tonight.

ELIZABETH: Looks like it might storm.

HORACE, SR.: I hope not. The crops don't need rain now.

BROTHER: Mama says you're going to have another baby?

ELIZABETH: Yes, I am.

BROTHER: Well I'll have to come back to see the new baby.

Big Horace, what did you pay for that rent house you bought from Papa?

HORACE, SR.: Five hundred dollars . . . Why?

BROTHER: I was going over the books again last week and I didn't see any record of it.

HORACE, SR.: I bought it when I sold my Liberty Bonds. I paid cash for it. I have a receipt if you want to see it.

BROTHER: No. No. I was just curious when I couldn't find any record of it at all.

HORACE, SR.: I'm sure there's a record there somewhere.

BROTHER: How much rent do you get for it?

HORACE, SR.: Ten dollars a month, but the tenants I have have only been able to pay two months' rent so far.

BROTHER: How long have they been there?

HORACE, SR.: Seven months.

BROTHER: I'd kick them out if they didn't pay.

HORACE, SR.: I can't do that. They say they'll pay when they have the money.

BROTHER: They never will. I wish you'd look at Papa's books. The rent that's owed him on the Gossett house and the brick buildings . . . month after month. Only trash rents. They never pay, no matter what they promise, because they never have any money. They have absolutely no ambition. The same with the tenants out on the farms. They've been there too long. They think they can stay on forever and do absolutely nothing and Mama will always keep them. I don't believe in that kind of sentiment. I absolutely don't. I would get rid of them all. Oh, I'd give them warning, but I would say that if they didn't straighten out and start working and making crops . . . I would absolutely . . . (*Pause.*) Yes, I guess I would. (*He laughs.*) Look who's talking. A man that has never made a living for himself in his life. A man that has had everything given to him and has done nothing but waste it all. I tell you, I wish I had been born with nothing. I wish I'd had to make my way from the day I was born. I wish my father had had nothing and that to keep alive I'd had to work from morning to night in the fields in the sun . . . I wish . . . (*He sees the picture.*) Who's this?

HORACE, SR.: My father and my mother.

BROTHER: You don't look like him.

HORACE, SR.: No.

BROTHER: I don't look a thing like Papa either. (*Looks again at the picture.*) He must have been a young man when this was taken.

HORACE, SR.: I think so.

BROTHER (*looking on back of picture*): Here. It says he was twenty-one. Your mother was eighteen.

HORACE, SR.: That's about right.

BROTHER: I'm pleased with how Papa's picture turned out, aren't you?

ELIZABETH: Oh, yes, I am.

BROTHER: Considering it was only a Kodak to start with. I think Mr. Howard did an excellent job in cutting it down and enlarging it. (*Pause.*) I warn you, Mama has some scheme about me going into a grocery store because Papa used to have one. She thinks I might do well as a merchant, now I've failed as a farmer. But don't let her talk me into it. Make her take what money she has left and invest it with that Houston Trust Company.

ELIZABETH: How much does she have left, Brother?

BROTHER: Oh, she has something. Not as much as she once had, but there's something.

ELIZABETH: Have you been able to collect much of the money owed Papa?

BROTHER: No. People are terrible, you know. They find excuse after excuse not to pay their debts. They seem to think all debts should be canceled out at Papa's death. Everything. And you know Mama is no help. If I want to turn them over to a lawyer, she won't let me. She makes an excuse for this one and for that one. So . . . nothing has been collected. (*Pause.*) And in all honesty, I haven't kept at it. You need someone with determination who will go back week after week. Pin them down. That's not me.

ELIZABETH: How much is owed us?

BROTHER: I can't tell you right off, Sister. It's a lot. Maybe fifteen thousand dollars. We'll be lucky at this rate if we collect three . . . (*He gets up.*) I'm tired. I'm going to bed early. (*He goes.*)

HORACE, JR.: Why does everybody talk about money all the time?

HORACE, SR.: You're going to learn why when you grow up and have to make a living.

ELIZABETH: Don't be so cross, Horace.

HORACE, SR.: He gets me mad. He's always getting into things that are none of his business. (*He gets up and leaves as the lights fade.*)

(*The lights are brought up upstage left.* MRS. VAUGHN *is there in a dressing gown in a chair.* HORACE, JR., *comes in.*)

HORACE, JR.: How do you feel?

MRS. VAUGHN: Better. I'm breathing easier today. They tell me you started to work today taking your daddy his dinner.

HORACE, JR.: Yes Ma'am. (*Pause.*) Did you hear about Gertrude?

MRS. VAUGHN: Yes, Eliza is over at the house now. She was her niece. She drowned, didn't she?

HORACE, JR.: In Caney Creek. She was in a boat and it turned over and she couldn't swim.

MRS. VAUGHN: Poor thing.

HORACE, JR.: She wanted to be a teacher or a nurse. She was going to Prairie Creek Normal to college.

MRS. VAUGHN: Poor creature.

HORACE, JR.: Are you going to her funeral?

MRS. VAUGHN: No.

HORACE, JR.: I wanted to go but Mama says I'm too young. She wouldn't even let me go to Papa's funeral. I saw Papa dead in his room, though. Remember?

MRS. VAUGHN: I do.

HORACE, JR.: Where is Brother?

MRS. VAUGHN: He's in his room. He's not well today either.

ELIZA (*coming in*): I'm back.

MRS. VAUGHN: You didn't have to come home today. You should be with your people today. They need you.

ELIZA: I knew you were sick here.

MRS. VAUGHN: I can manage. You go on back now.

ELIZA: Thank you. (*She starts out.*)

HORACE, JR.: When's the funeral going to be?

ELIZA: Day after tomorrow.

HORACE, JR.: Mama is going to send some flowers.

ELIZA: Everybody is being real kind. (*She goes out.*)

HORACE, JR.: Can you swim?

MRS. VAUGHN: No.

HORACE, JR.: Neither can I. My daddy learned to swim in the river. He said he just jumped in and taught himself. He says the river is not safe to go near now. The raft has made suck holes and there are alligators and poisonous snakes everywhere. Mama says she won't have me go near the river.

MRS. VAUGHN: Your grandfather worked so hard to have something done about that raft damming up the river.

HORACE, JR.: Which grandfather?

MRS. VAUGHN: Papa.

HORACE, JR.: Oh. I have another grandfather, you know, too.

MRS. VAUGHN: Of course, you do.

HORACE, JR.: He's dead, too.

MRS. VAUGHN: I know he is, honey.

HORACE, JR.: Did you go to his funeral?

MRS. VAUGHN: No. Not that I remember.

HORACE, JR.: Did he have a big funeral?

MRS. VAUGHN: I'm sure he did.

HORACE, JR.: As big as Papa's?

MRS. VAUGHN: I don't know, honey. I doubt if he did, though.

HORACE, JR.: I doubt it, too. Nobody has ever had that big a funeral.

MRS. VAUGHN: He was very loved.

WALTER (coming in): Mrs. Vaughn, could I ask a favor of you, please? Eliza was supposed to ask you but she didn't know how to. Could you advance us some money, please, Ma'am?

MRS. VAUGHN: How much?

WALTER: A hundred dollars . . .

MRS. VAUGHN: A hundred dollars? What do you need so much for?

WALTER: For Gertrude's funeral. Her mama don't have the money to buy a casket and to bury her.

MRS. VAUGHN: Oh . . . Get me my checkbook.

(He does so. She writes out a check.)

This is a gift from me. I want to pay for the funeral.

WALTER: No Ma'am. We didn't . . .

MRS. VAUGHN: I want to. Just don't say anything about it. You just go on like you and Eliza are doing it.

WALTER: Yes'm. (*To* HORACE, JR.:) You want me to take you over to see Gertrude? Your mama said I could. She's coming over later this afternoon. She thinks Henry Vaughn is too young to go, but she said I could bring you over with me. I'll bring you right back.

HORACE, JR.: Sure.

(*They go out as the lights fade.*)

(*The lights are brought up on the living room.* HORACE, SR., *is there reading the paper.* MRS. VAUGHN *comes in.*)

MRS. VAUGHN: Has Elizabeth come back from Gertrude's funeral yet?

HORACE, SR.: No. How do you feel?

MRS. VAUGHN: Much better. Brother drove down to Galveston last night.

HORACE, SR.: Did he? For a vacation?

MRS. VAUGHN: No. He's going to see about a job as a merchant seaman.

HORACE, SR.: Oh, yes. I remember his talking about that.

MRS. VAUGHN: What do you think of his leaving?

HORACE, SR.: I don't know.

MRS. VAUGHN: I think he's just running away from his

troubles, myself. I told him that but he doesn't agree. I offered to loan him the money to buy a grocery business, but he didn't want to do it. I went down to the office this afternoon. Nothing has been attended to and I don't know where to turn. (*Pause.*) I haven't mentioned this to Elizabeth, but I'm thinking of leaving here.

HORACE, SR.: What will you do?

MRS. VAUGHN: Travel. I'd go out to California and visit my sister there. I'd stay with my sister in Houston. I'd go to Dallas and visit Laura and go to New York and visit Dora while she's in school there. (*Pause.*) To tell you the truth, I might even in time sell my house here and live in Dallas or Houston. (*Pause.*) May I speak frankly with you?

HORACE, SR.: Yes Ma'am.

MRS. VAUGHN: I hear you owe the bank money?

HORACE, SR.: Yes Ma'am.

MRS. VAUGHN: And that you need to extend your note. If you're worried . . .

HORACE, SR.: Yes Ma'am. I was. But that's behind me now for another six months. They are extending my note.

MRS. VAUGHN: I want you to let me help you out. Let me loan you the money. You pay the bank off and you can pay me back when it's easy for you.

HORACE, SR.: I'm sorry but I can't accept it from you.

MRS. VAUGHN: You mustn't be like this!

HORACE, SR.: I just can't. I'm sorry.

MRS. VAUGHN: I'm sorry, too, because I was going to ask you to do something for me.

HORACE, SR.: What is it?

MRS. VAUGHN: If I go away I'll have no peace unless there is someone I can trust looking after my affairs. There's money still to be collected and the farms and the rents to be attended to. Would you consider taking over for me? Don't give me your answer now. You speak to Elizabeth and we'll talk again tomorrow.

HORACE, SR.: Do you think you'll be happy living away from here?

MRS. VAUGHN: I don't see why not. My children are all grown; they don't need me anymore. This isn't my home. I wasn't born here. I didn't come here until I was twenty. I was considered an old maid. Mr. Vaughn was twenty-six and he was considered as an old bachelor. He was tax collector and I worked for him over at the courthouse. I was the first woman to ever work a typewriter in the courthouse.

(ELIZABETH *comes in.*)

Is the funeral over?

ELIZABETH: Yes. Eliza says she'll be back in the morning to fix breakfast.

MRS. VAUGHN: Brother's gone to Galveston.

ELIZABETH: Is he?

(*She cries.* HORACE, JR., *goes to her.*)

HORACE, JR.: What's the matter, Mama?

ELIZABETH: Nothing. It's just that they have so little. Gertrude was always so happy and kind to you children. Life doesn't seem very fair to me sometimes. We have so much and they have so little.

HORACE, JR.: I thought we were poor.

ELIZABETH: We're certainly not poor, honey. Not like they are, anyway. They have nothing.

MRS. VAUGHN: Do you think you can find another nurse? You'll need someone for sure now with another baby on the way.

ELIZABETH: There was a cousin of Gertrude's there that seemed like a kind girl. Eliza said she would speak to her.

MRS. VAUGHN: Eliza might be available soon.

ELIZABETH: Why?

MRS. VAUGHN: I may close up the house and travel. Maybe she could work over here for you until I decide about the house. I'd pay their salaries.

ELIZABETH: We'll see.

MRS. VAUGHN: I've been disappointed with people here since your papa died. Why, they don't seem to remember him at all, or what he did for them and the town, and that hurts me. It's difficult sometimes for me not to remind them of their promises, but I've too much pride. When Brother told me of how Mr. Will Borden had cheated him about the cattle, I was so resentful I did go to the phone and I called his house. But fortunately he was not there and the next morning when he returned my call I made up some trivial thing to ask him about. But it does hurt when friends act so. And it hurts when they pave the road out there and cut down that pecan tree that when Papa gave them the land for the road he made them promise they would never touch it.

ELIZABETH: Did he have it in writing?

MRS. VAUGHN: No. But they promised him. I remember.

ELIZABETH: It is too bad it's not in writing.

MRS. VAUGHN: He had so little in writing. Half the money owed him he has only the notation in his ledger book and he never bothered to get people to sign notes. That's always how he did business. His word and their word . . . and now, of course, most of them pretend they don't remember. They ask where is the note they signed? Or they tell a worse lie. They say, "We paid him back" and if you ask for the receipt they say, "Since there was no note I naturally asked for no receipt." Anyway, I don't want to sit here nursing grievances and my resentments, and that's why I think I'll go away for a while. (*Pause.*) I've asked Horace, Elizabeth, to take over my affairs while I'm gone. To see to these debts owed us, for one thing. Brother couldn't cope with them at all.

HORACE, SR.: I don't know what I can do either.

MRS. VAUGHN: What time is it?

ELIZABETH: Near six.

MRS. VAUGHN: Brother is supposed to call me from Galveston to tell me his plans. I'd better go on home and wait for his call. (*She leaves.*)

ELIZABETH: There's not much for supper.

HORACE, SR.: That's all right. I'm not too hungry. Horace, Jr., go see if your grandmother has gone.

HORACE, JR. (*looking out*): Yes Sir. She's going through the backyard now.

HORACE, SR.: I didn't know how to tell her; the sheriff came by the store just before closing time to tell me the Galveston officers had called him. They have Brother in jail there. He got drunk and he stabbed a man. The man died. I thought you should be the one to tell your mother.

ELIZABETH: I can't tell her.

HORACE, SR.: Yes, you can.

ELIZABETH: I can't. I can't. I can't. She's had to bear so much.

(*She is crying.* MRS. VAUGHN *comes quietly into the room.*)

MRS. VAUGHN: I left my purse.

(*She notices* ELIZABETH *is crying.*)

What's wrong? Why are you crying?

ELIZABETH: It's about Brother. He's in trouble again, Mama. He got drunk in Galveston and he stabbed a man. The man died.

MRS. VAUGHN: Well . . . that is trouble. Horace, Jr., I see Walter's light on in his house. Go tell him I want him to drive me to Galveston right away.

HORACE, JR.: Yes Ma'am. (*He runs off.*)

MRS. VAUGHN: Will you go with me, Elizabeth?

ELIZABETH: If you'd like me to.

MRS. VAUGHN: Yes, I would. (*Pause.*) Your papa used to say, "I wonder what would happen if we didn't help

Brother out of this?" He and I often thought . . . maybe
. . . maybe . . .

(*She turns to them.*)

How can I help him? I would leave him in jail until his trial
if I thought that would help him. Do you think it would?
What if your son got drunk and stabbed a man in Galveston and was in jail, what would you do? Would you
leave him there on the chance that it would help him? Or
would you go to him, hoping . . .

(ELIZABETH *starts out.*)

ELIZABETH: I'm going to get ready. (*She leaves.*)

MRS. VAUGHN: Help me, Horace. I turn to you. What
should I do? What would you do?

HORACE, SR.: I don't know. I only know when I got into
trouble there was no one I could turn to to help me out.

MRS. VAUGHN: And was that a blessing in disguise, do you
think?

HORACE, SR.: I don't know now. There was a time I felt
very bitter about it. I felt no one cared about me at all.
Now I don't know.

HORACE, JR. (*coming in*): Walter says he's ready when you
are. Can I go with you?

HORACE, SR.: No, Son. This is no time for you to be going.

MRS. VAUGHN (*starting out*): Tell Elizabeth we'll be by in
the car in about half an hour. (*She continues on.*)

HORACE, JR.: Miss Ida knows Uncle Brother killed a man.

She saw me in the yard just now and she asked me how my grandmother was taking it.

HORACE, SR.: I'm sure everybody in town knows by now. I wish I could pick up and leave. I wish I could travel to California.

HORACE, JR.: Why?

HORACE, SR.: Because I'm sick and tired of people and their curiosity. They always come to me when they want to find out something about the Vaughns. They nearly drove me crazy after Mr. Vaughn's death trying to find out the size of his estate, and then when Brother was in charge—every time he was drunk someone would come by the store to let me know he knew Brother wasn't attending to his father's business. Tomorrow I'll have fifty visitors with a million questions. How did it happen? How did your grandmother take it?

(*Pause.*)

HORACE, JR.: It's raining.

HORACE, SR.: It sure is. The poor cotton crop. (*He goes and looks out the window.*) I don't like your mother driving at night in the rain. The roads will be terrible if it keeps up.

HORACE, JR.: Do you get wet when you are in the grave-yard when it rains?

HORACE, SR.: What?

HORACE, JR.: When you are buried in the graveyard do you get wet when it rains?

HORACE, SR.: What made you think of that?

HORACE, JR.: Gertrude. I was wondering about her.

HORACE, SR.: Oh . . . (*He starts away.*)

HORACE, JR.: Where are you going?

HORACE, SR.: To find your mother. (*He starts away.*)

HORACE, JR.: Daddy . . .

HORACE, SR.: Yes?

HORACE, JR. (*going to him*): I have to tell you something. I'm scared.

HORACE, SR.: Of what?

HORACE, JR.: I saw a dove on our house today. I took a rock and chucked at it, but it wouldn't go away.

HORACE, SR.: Oh, Son, you're too old now to believe in foolishness like that. That means nothing at all. Nothing, nothing at all.

(*He holds his son close to him and takes him offstage as the lights fade. The lights are brought up down left. INEZ and CORELLA are there. HORACE, JR., enters.*)

HORACE, JR.: When are Mother and Daddy going to get here?

CORELLA: It shouldn't be long. Did you ride your horse today?

HORACE, JR.: No. I couldn't. He has a sore leg.

INEZ: I think he rides that horse too fast.

CORELLA: Did you hear what your auntie said? You ride your horse too fast.

(*He doesn't answer. He gets a book and begins to read.*)

I prayed every night he would have given up reading those books by the time I came back here on a visit. But my prayers weren't answered. (*Pause.*) Son, you still read too much. Your big mama was hoping you had quit that now that you had a horse and you were working at the store with your daddy. You can't read at the store, can you?

HORACE, JR.: Yes, I can when we're not busy. Which is most of the time. Daddy said you'd go crazy if you couldn't read. It's either that or talk to all the idlers in town that come in every five minutes to ask about Uncle Brother and his trial.

CORELLA (*to* INEZ): The phone didn't stop ringing once last night. Everybody in town was calling to see what the verdict was. I swear, I think half of them were disappointed when I said he was acquitted.

ELIZA (*coming in*): Little Horace, go out in the sandpile and play with your brother. I have a big dinner to cook.

HORACE, JR.: I don't want to play with him.

ELIZA: Your mother said for you to. Now, get out there.

HORACE, JR.: I'm too big for him. Get somebody his own age to play with him.

CORELLA: Now mind, Horace, Jr. You go keep him happy and content.

(*He starts out with the book.*)

Now, you leave that book here. You'll get to reading the book and Henry Vaughn will wander off to the river and drown.

HORACE, JR.: I wish he would.

ELIZA: What did you say?

CORELLA: Now, he didn't mean that. Did you, Horace, Jr.?

HORACE, JR.: No Ma'am. I guess not.

(*He puts the book down and goes outside.* ELIZA *follows after him.*)

INEZ: I don't guess big Horace will try to go to the store again today.

CORELLA: I hope not. He'll be worn out after that trip from Galveston. Depending on the roads it will take them three to four hours. They were going to try to get off by seven this morning, Elizabeth said. I'm glad Horace got a little change. I think he looks terrible. I know he's working too hard. He leaves for the store at seven every morning and he's not back here until six-thirty at night. He doesn't even close it for a noon meal. And now he has the responsibility of Mary's estate. He says that has him nearly half crazy.

INEZ: Why?

CORELLA: He didn't tell me why. You know he never discusses his affairs with me. If I want to learn anything about him or the family I have to ask Elizabeth. But I have all the same a pretty good idea why. I think he thinks Mary is too extravagant and is going to land in the poorhouse.

INEZ: I wonder what it cost her to get Brother out of his scrape?

CORELLA: I don't know that it cost her anything.

INEZ: Now, you know it did. (*Whispering.*) Some people think it must have cost her as much as ten thousand dollars.

CORELLA: Oh, my God! No wonder he's worried. On Saturdays he opens the store at seven in the morning and doesn't close until ten-thirty at night. He said he wouldn't mind the long hours if he were only busy. He says the lack of business is what drives him crazy. At least, that's what Elizabeth tells me. Like I say, he doesn't tell me anything.

INEZ: You know, sometimes he offends people. Mrs. Carter said he offended her.

CORELLA: How?

INEZ: Well, she went in to buy something and he was waiting on a colored man and there was a colored woman waiting, too. And he finished waiting on the colored man and then he waited on the colored woman. So Mrs. Carter walked out.

CORELLA: Mrs. Carter is a fool.

(HORACE, JR., *comes in and gets his book.*)

I also heard her say at your house she didn't know why Mrs. Henry Vaughn was so stuck up: everybody knew she had been Mr. Vaughn's secretary before they married. I felt like telling her, too, that we all knew her father was a saloon keeper in Houston's Fifth Ward before she married.

(INEZ *gives her a look and points to* HORACE, JR.)

Horace, Jr., did you hear what I just said?

HORACE, JR.: What did you just say?

CORELLA: Never mind. But if you heard it, don't you dare repeat it.

HORACE, JR.: Which part don't you want me to repeat? About my grandmother or about Mrs. Carter?

CORELLA: Neither. Where is your brother?

HORACE, JR.: Eliza got Sarah to take him visiting.

CORELLA: Poor little thing. They just push him around so.

(ELIZABETH *and* HORACE, SR., *come in.*)

Well . . . I'm glad to see you. I know you're tired.

ELIZABETH: We are.

HORACE, SR.: What time is dinner, Mama?

CORELLA: Eliza planned it for twelve.

HORACE, SR. (*looking at his watch*): I'm just going down quickly and check on things at the store before dinner.

ELIZABETH: Miss Corrie, will you and Miss Inez have dinner with us?

CORELLA: Oh, I think your family should be alone. You don't want company today.

ELIZABETH: Stay and have dinner at least.

CORELLA: Where's your mother?

ELIZABETH: She and Brother went on over to the house. They're not having dinner.

CORELLA: Well, all right.

HORACE, JR.: What's so bad about working in the Fifth Ward in Houston?

HORACE, SR.: Because it's the toughest ward there. Why?

HORACE, JR.: Nothing. I just wondered.

ELIZA (*coming in*): Mrs. Vaughn sent Walter over that she and Brother were coming for dinner after all and that they would like to have it as soon as possible as they are leaving right after dinner for Houston. I have everything ready to serve if it's all right with you.

ELIZABETH: It is with me.

CORELLA: I don't think we'll stay, after all. Do you think Walter could drive us to town? We'll eat there.

ELIZABETH: I'm sure. Eliza, ask Walter to drive Miss Corrie and Miss Inez to town.

ELIZA: I will.

(*She leaves.* CORELLA *gets up and kisses her daughter-in-law and her son.*)

CORELLA: I'm glad everything turned out all right for your family.

ELIZABETH: Thank you so much for coming and helping us out.

CORELLA: I'm glad to help anytime I can. (*She kisses her son again.*) Don't work too hard, Son. You look very peaked to me. Are you worried?

HORACE, SR.: Of course I'm worried, Mama. Everybody worries sometimes.

INEZ: Not me. I refuse to worry. Because it doesn't do one bit of good.

CORELLA: I tell you what worries me. Seeing that child

with his nose stuck in a book constantly. When I was here last time I reminded you about Terrence Robedaux.

HORACE, SR.: I know you did, Mama. But if that's all I had to worry about, my son reading so much, I would be a happy man.

CORELLA: I think overeducation is a curse. I can name you boy after boy that were overeducated like Terrence Robedaux and weren't worth killing.

HORACE, SR.: And I can name you boy after boy whose family had no interest at all in them or what they learned. Who no one cared if they went to school or if they didn't. What they had to bear, what they had . . . And those boys . . . most of them . . . a great many of them, are not worth much today either . . . And some of them that did survive have to work like dogs to make ends meet and to make up for their total lack of education. I could tell you heart-breaking stories, too, about those boys. And if I have to choose between the two for my son . . . I will choose . . .

(WALTER *comes in.*)

CORELLA: Elizabeth, I swear I didn't mean a thing in this world. He is so sensitive. I swear I don't know why he is so sensitive.

WALTER: You all ready?

INEZ: Yes, we are.

CORELLA: I only meant what I said in the kindest way. I didn't mean for a second to upset him.

ELIZABETH: I know.

CORELLA: Please tell him that.

ELIZABETH: I will.

(CORELLA *and* INEZ *leave.*)

HORACE, JR.: Do you know what Mrs. Carter said about Grandmother? She said she didn't know why she was so stuck-up . . . because . . .

ELIZABETH: Tell me some other time, Son.

MRS. VAUGHN (*coming in*): Thank you for having your dinner early. Brother and I have made a decision. He's taking a vow never to drink again and I'm going to rent the house here and we'll go this afternoon to Dallas and stay with Laura until we can rent a house there and he can look around there for a job or find a small business to buy and make a fresh start. He says he can't bring himself to go uptown here, he's too ashamed. Well, I told him I'm glad he's ashamed. Because that's certainly better than acting like Teddy Murdock did after he was acquitted for killing T. J. Rowe . . . walking up and down the street and shaking hands and being congratulated by his friends. Brother says Harrison and his associates here since childhood have been his undoing. Of course, he admits he was weak himself or he would never have allowed others to lead him astray. But he says he has at last learned his lesson and that he will seek out the finest type of young men to associate with in Dallas. And I must say, at last, I believe him.

(ELIZABETH *doesn't answer. There is silence.* HORACE, SR., *doesn't answer.*)

Horace, Sr., tell me I'm doing the right thing. I'm scared to death. I want so to do the right thing for him. (*Pause.*) You don't think I'm doing the right thing?

HORACE, SR.: I didn't say that. I can't tell you what to do. Because I don't know what is the right thing.

MRS. VAUGHN: If he were your boy, what would you do?

HORACE, SR.: He's not my boy. And if he were . . . (*Pause.*) I wouldn't know what to do any more than you do.

MRS. VAUGHN: You know something? You used to drink and gamble as a young man. You were wild and you got into trouble. You know I know that. That's why we didn't want Elizabeth to marry you. We were frightened that you . . . (*Pause.*) But you've changed. You're responsible and hardworking. A good husband and father. How have you changed?

HORACE, SR.: I don't know. I just did. I loved Elizabeth and I did.

MRS. VAUGHN: You see, Mr. Vaughn could never understand his own son because he never did any of these things. He went to work at twelve. He took care of his mother and his brother and his sisters. He put himself through college. He graduated with honors. He went into business right away and was a successful businessman by the time he was thirty. He simply could never understand Brother behaving so. (*Pause.*) We'll go visit your papa's grave before we leave. Promise to go out there once or twice a week and see that the flowers stay watered.

ELIZABETH: I will.

BROTHER (*coming in*): Are we going to eat soon?

ELIZABETH: Any time you all are ready. (*She gets up. She starts out.*) I'll help Eliza get it on the table. (*She goes.*)

BROTHER: I'll wait outside until it's ready.

MRS. VAUGHN: I think it's ready now. They're putting it on the table.

BROTHER: I want to wait outside. I want to go out and look one last time at the yard. I've spent twenty-eight years of my life here, and I may never see it again.

MRS. VAUGHN: You'll see it again, I'm sure.

BROTHER: Look at Mama and envy her. I don't believe you have an ounce of sentiment, Mama. Here you are leaving the house you raised your children in, maybe for good, and you act like we're going on an afternoon ride to the farms.

MRS. VAUGHN: How else can one act? I never look back.

BROTHER: When you left your home and moved here . . . did you ever think of one day returning?

MRS. VAUGHN: Never. My mother and father left the plantation, too, soon after. I couldn't even find it now if my life depended on it.

BROTHER: You never think about it?

MRS. VAUGHN: Never.

BROTHER: And Papa? You never think of him?

MRS. VAUGHN: That's cruel and unkind, Brother. Not a day passes that I don't think of your papa. I adored your papa. I worshiped your papa.

BROTHER: I know you did.

MRS. VAUGHN: But we have to go on, you know. On and on and on. I'll tell you something. The day he died I prayed all that night to be taken and I meant my prayers. But they weren't answered, and I'm living on. And I have to do the best I can. And don't think you're the only reason I'm leaving. Ask Elizabeth, I have thought often of traveling. Going to California to visit my sisters. (*Pause.*) Maybe we should go to California and find a business for you.

BROTHER: No. You go to California if you like. I don't want to leave Texas. (*He goes out to the center area. He stands looking around.*)

MRS. VAUGHN: He loves this place. He loves his home. He said to me just now: "Mama, what is wrong with me? I love my home. Why can't I live on here?" And he talks all the time now about his papa. You know, like he was doing coming back in the car from Galveston. How unfair it was. A fine man like your papa had to die. I know what he means, poor boy, that he is living and not worth much. You remember, he said as much to me coming home in the car. Did you ever have doubts about your worth, Horace?

HORACE, SR.: Yes Ma'am.

ELIZABETH (*coming in*): Everything's ready.

HORACE, SR.: I'll get Brother.

(*He goes out to* BROTHER. ELIZABETH *and her mother go out.*)

HORACE, SR. (*calling*): Brother . . .

BROTHER: Yes.

HORACE, SR.: Dinner.

BROTHER: Thank you. How long were you on the road?

HORACE, SR.: Nine months. I went all over four states:

Texas, Louisiana, Mississippi, Arkansas, and parts of Alabama.

BROTHER: Do you think I'm doing the right thing going?

HORACE, SR.: I don't give advice.

BROTHER: Maybe one day I'll be able to come back. This is my home, but I can't live in my home. I have to wander . . . because that's what I feel I'll be doing. I told Mama I'm going to Dallas to start a business, but I'll never stay in Dallas. (*Pause.*) How much did it cost Mama to get me off?

HORACE, SR.: I don't know.

BROTHER: Did it cost her anything?

HORACE, SR.: I don't know.

BROTHER: I'll stay in Dallas a week or so to get a little rest and then I'll go to New Orleans and sign onto a boat there.

ELIZABETH (*coming out*): Aren't you all coming in? Your dinner is getting cold.

(HORACE, SR., *and* BROTHER *start into the house.*)

BROTHER: I used to feel so sorry for you when you would come and call on Elizabeth. I'd hear Papa and Mama talking and they said you were practically an orphan and had no home. Now you have a home and I don't. I expect someday you'll even be living in my home while I'm wandering around the world.

HORACE, SR.: No, I won't. This is my home.

BROTHER: Don't be too sure. Don't be too sure about anything, big Horace. Not about anything in this world.

(*They continue on as the lights fade.*)

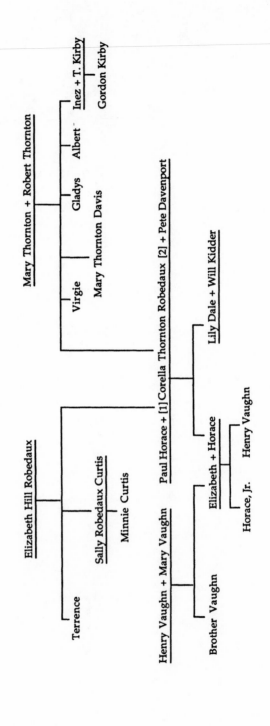